Praise for *Kindred Souls*

A "gift from God," a "vocation of lo~
of those whose hearts burn as t'
journey: this is the territory Step₁   ₁ ner
lovely book, *Kindred Souls*. Rooting   ₁n scripture and drawing on a rich ecumeni⸱   ⸱ of witnesses,
Ford shows us in fresh and inviting wayₛ that friendship—
between those who love God, between the living and those
already departed, between God-seekers and God's self—is
a vital and essential part of the Christian life.

—WENDY M. WRIGHT, PhD
Professor of Theology, Creighton University
Omaha, Nebraska

Kindred Souls makes a significant contribution to literature
on spiritual friendship. Stephanie Ford writes out of rich
personal experience, but she has securely anchored her
study in scriptures, Christian history, and sound theology
and psychology. Persons and groups looking for ways to
deepen relationships with others should turn to this sensi-
tive and wise book; it's a delight to read.

—E. GLENN HINSON
Professor Emeritus of Spirituality and
John Loftis Professor of Church History
Baptist Theological Seminary at Richmond, Virginia

Kindred Souls

Connecting Through Spiritual Friendship

STEPHANIE FORD

UPPER ROOM BOOKS®
NASHVILLE

Cover design: Thelma Whitworth/TMW Designs
Cover image: © SuperStock
Interior design: Nancy Terzian/Nter Design
First printing: 2006

Library of Congress Cataloging-in-Publication
Ford, Stephanie, 1959–
Kindred souls : connecting through spiritual friendship / Stephanie Ford.
    p. cm.
Includes bibliographical references.
ISBN-13: 978-0-8358-9903-1
ISBN-10: 0-8358-9903-9
1. Friendship—Religious aspects—Christianity. I. Title.
BV4647.F7F67 2006
241'.6762—dc22

                      2006030001

In memory of my spiritual mentor
and beloved aunt
Betty Lide Fletcher (1928–87)

Contents

Acknowledgments

This book was conceived out of a series of talks I offered at a twentieth reunion gathering of the Academy for Spiritual Formation at Camp Sumatanga, Alabama, in July 2002. I am grateful to Jerry Haas, whose invitation to speak on the topic was the springboard. It was indeed rich to meditate on spiritual friendship and to participate in dialogue with the delightful community of souls gathered at Sumatanga.

I am most grateful to the fine editors of Upper Room Books. Lynne Deming provided encouragement both through timely e-mails and in person. Anne Trudel was gracious and flexible as we worked on editing the final manuscript. Thanks also to JoAnn Miller for her early guidance on the project and to Denise Duke for her careful documentation checks.

I feel blessed to have parents who gave me a passion for the spiritual life: my father, a thoughtful professor of philosophy and religion; and my mother, a lay teacher of faith as well as a leader of prayer and healing groups. They have greatly encouraged me in this endeavor. As I share in the first chapter, my sister, Rachel, was my first spiritual friend. I learned much about true friendship from her. Now she teaches me what it means to be a good mother, and I am grateful for her tutorials and companionship in this new venture of parenting.

I give thanks for spiritual friends who have opened their hearts to me with compassion, good humor, courage, and a willingness to trust me with the truth of their own lives— just as they have received my own soul's truth. Although I am a romantic, I realize that friendship has been the abiding treasure of my life. In writing this book I was helped in particular ways. Thanks to Paul and Sue Stroud for a life-changing conversation at their dinner table; to Shelley Newby, whose pilgrimage of faith opened new meanings for me in the story of Ruth and Naomi; to Doug Gwyn for the gift of his rich sermon series "Conversations with Christ," and to Mary Moore for her faithful companionship in the sacred task of writing.

I count my husband, Les, as a dear spiritual companion. Les was also my first editor! Faithfully he read every chapter, cheering me on through the doldrums of late nights at the computer and helping me to think through my approach to each topic. His skillful editing meant that the initial draft I submitted to Upper Room Books was much more polished than any I could have submitted on my own.

Finally, I want to thank the dean and faculty of the Earlham School of Religion for the sabbatical time for this project and to acknowledge Michael Birkel of Earlham College, who inspired me through his literary friendship with the eighteenth-century Quaker reformer John Woolman to consider the vitality of my own friendships within the communion of saints. Two of these living saints are E. Glenn Hinson and Anne Thomas Neil, both pioneers in Baptist spirituality. Echoes of their mentoring reverberate continually in my life and vocation.

Preface

Friendship is both a gift and a mystery. Sometimes a rich connection is made in moments; other relationships begin unspectacularly but develop into lifelong, faithful friendships. We may feel eternal bonds with persons quite unlike us in temperament, while once important friendships fade over time. When we consider those kindred souls who have graced our lives, we soon realize that there is no one-size-fits-all approach to friendship.

In this book I wonder with you, the reader, about the nature and calling of true spiritual friendship. Through spiritual encounters with others, I have been profoundly transformed, and I treasure the kindred souls with whom I share the journey. These friendships call me to prayer, to authenticity and growth, to self-compassion, and to greater faithfulness in my walk with Christ. And just as the spiritual practices I value also require, these soul kinships ask certain things of me: time, intention, loyalty, and disciplines like good listening and patience.

In chapter 1 we begin by exploring a definition of spiritual friendship, its parameters and significance. What makes a spiritual friendship distinctive? What signs show that a spiritual kinship is emerging? What are the unique qualities and tools needed to support such a friendship? What can our earliest spiritual connections teach us about the ways of true friendship?

Chapter 2 looks back through the centuries of Christian tradition for resources informing genuine spiritual friendship. Aelred of Rievaulx, a twelfth-century English abbot, wrote the first Christian treatise on the subject. He describes the qualities of a true friendship grounded in Christ. Living in Italy around the same time as Aelred but probably unaware of his writings were Francis and Clare of Assisi. Their friendship offers an exemplary model of the qualities Aelred espouses. Chapter 2 also considers possibilities for nurturing friendship across time within the communion of saints.

In chapter 3 we reflect on Ruth and Naomi as biblical witnesses to an amazing story of friendship: two widows who forged an unexpected kinship of courage and loyal love. Their story invites us to ask certain questions: How are spiritual friendships a calling or vocation? What covenantal love does loyal friendship require? How might our spiritual friendships bear fruit in the world?

In chapter 4 we turn to the life of Jesus and his approach to friendship. We discover the radical nature of kingdom love that filled his friendships as time and again he reached out in friendship to those outside the social circle of a typical Jewish male. We witness Jesus' gifts for being fully present to the one before him, for asking the right question, and for reminding his followers that the kingdom of God is a table extending friendship to everyone.

Chapter 5 invites us to consider our first and most important friendship, our friendship with God. How do we come to know our first Friend and to deepen this relationship to Spirit and Mystery? How might the Trinity model divine friendship? How does Jesus' teaching in John 15 exemplify the ways of divine friendship? What does our partnership with God call us to offer to a needy world?

Finally, in chapter 6 we explore a few practical details of contemporary spiritual friendships. Overbooked schedules and the mobility of our society challenge friendships today. Nevertheless, the rich gifts of soul kinship are possible, even through distance. We consider the responsibilities inherent in the boundaries we are called to keep, as well as ways we may grow and sustain spiritual friendships in the contemporary context.

I hope and pray that through these pages you will find encouragement to deepen the soul friendships already present in your life, as well as to be attentive to new friendship possibilities God opens to you. Prayer partners may decide to read this book and discuss it as part of their weekly meetings. Soul companions of many years might want to take the text along on a weekend retreat as a companion for reflecting on their own friendship and envisioning the future. The book can easily serve as a guide for a six-week small group study on spiritual friendship, as each chapter provides several opportunities for discussion and journaling.

Spiritual friendship is both a gift of grace and a work of intention. Today, more than ever, we need to strengthen these bonds that carry a promise of eternal soul kinship.

CHAPTER 1

The Gift of
Spiritual Friendship

What is a spiritual friendship? What distinguishes a spiritual friendship from other kinds of friendship? Does a person have to be more religious to participate in such a friendship? These are good questions.

As we explore this important topic, consider what comes to mind when you think of the word *friend*. Perhaps somewhere boxed in the attic you have a pencil-smeared friendship pledge you wrote to your best friend in the third grade. Or, in your mind's eye, you see the face of a college buddy who helped you stay awake through all-night study sessions. Maybe you picture a coworker who reached out to you recently in care, bringing a pot of soup and some magazines when you were at home with the flu. You sensed the eagerness of a new friendship developing.

A myriad of faces and feelings may arise when you think of friendship. No doubt they include persons with whom you have shared certain sympathies—those with whom you have laughed, argued, and cried. You may also think of friends lost to the sweep of time in our ever-mobile culture. Memories of pain surface, hurts you have tried to forget.

Adding the modifier *spiritual* need not create a pious hedge around friendship. Rather, the word *spiritual* emphasizes the calling and depth of a faithful friendship grounded in relationship with God. Such a friendship is more than a relationship based on similar likes, overlapping interests and values, or even years in the same community. C. S. Lewis spoke about the nature of spiritual friendship, describing it as a friendship of "kindred souls"—two persons who care about the same truth. In Celtic Christian thinking, your soul friend—*anam cara*—is your companion who carries the truest mirror reflecting the light of your soul.

In my experience of soul kinship, I find I can speak my heart to a spiritual friend and trust that the other receives my words with care and prayerful regard. I can be myself and risk talking about feelings or ideas I may not have expressed anywhere else for fear of judgment. This does not mean that the friendship is superficial; I still crave true speaking from my friend, but I can trust that she or he will carefully consider words of challenge or concern to me. Over time, through a mutual bond born of faithful attention to the other, each of us may call the other to his or her own unique highest good.

Another characteristic of spiritual friendship is its nature of calling, even vocation. You sense the Spirit's leading to pursue a particular relationship. The biblical friendships of David and Jonathan, Ruth and Naomi, and Paul and Timothy speak to this understanding. Through such communities of two God's presence was realized in human form—in compassion and even prophetic change. For some the call may come in sparks kindled instantly between hearts—a knowing that can't be explained. Sometimes humor, an unexpected kindness, or a crisis draws two persons to each other, and only later, in reflection, does the true depth of the friendship come to light. Then there are slowly growing soul friendships that blossom over months, perhaps years. Whatever the case, a soul friendship is not only a gift from God but also a vocation of love to be tended with loyalty and care. Some friendships may even call upon one to sacrifice for the other, as Jonathan did for David.

In the Christian tradition, a fundamental characteristic of spiritual friendship is its grounding in Christ. In the Gospel of John, Jesus offers a profound testimony to spiritual friendship when he tells his disciples, "I do not call you servants any longer, because the servant does not know what the master is doing; but I have called you friends, because I have made known to you everything that I have

A fundamental characteristic of spiritual friendship is its grounding in Christ.

heard from my Father" (John 15:15). How moving it must have been for the disciples to hear their beloved teacher elevate their status to the level of friends. In this teachable moment Jesus points beyond himself to the Source of his befriending love. He names the Third One present in their midst—the Father. Likewise, we in turn, as God's offspring through Christ, acknowledge that Christ is the unseen mediator who dwells at the center of our kinship with others. Christ is the one who invites us into deeper communion with the Divine through the common experience of human encounter.

Jesus drew his disciples into spiritual friendship over a three-year ministry. But we also witness significant one-time meetings between Jesus and seekers like Nicodemus and the Samaritan woman. Can we call such brief encounters spiritual friendship? I think so. Deep friendships can emerge in spaces as small as hours and moments.

The 1985 movie *The Trip to Bountiful* tells the story of an elderly woman confined to a small apartment in Houston with her only son and a prickly daughter-in-law in the early days of World War II. Longing to return to her home place—an abandoned farm in Bountiful, Texas—the elderly Carrie runs away from her children and sets out for Bountiful by bus with a small pension check. Her seatmate is a young woman whose husband has recently been deployed by the military. Carrie quickly warms up to her pretty companion, Thelma, and begins sharing stories from childhood and singing bits of hymns, recalling her first lost love and remembering the beauty of her home place.

Carrie's eyes sparkle as she shares her heart with the empathetic Thelma. Carrie also listens lovingly to the stories of her young friend. Finally Carrie trusts Thelma with the secret of her trip: she has escaped from her children to try living with an old friend in Bountiful again. In the brief span of an overnight bus ride, a spiritual friendship develops from the caring, loving listening of one stranger to another. As destinations would demand, the two travelers part—the climax of the story still ahead—but we are left with a picture of a true spiritual kinship, rich with layers that otherwise might have taken months or years to develop.

In the language of Jungian psychology, these unexpected holy moments and chance meetings are "synchronicities," experiences when the soul is mirrored in outer reality. They are sacred coincidences, not consciously orchestrated. In Christian understanding such encounters are considered Spirit-led and therefore abound with mystical potential.

Returning to our definition of spiritual friendship, we begin to see all sorts of possibilities. Rich soul kinships can emerge among persons of different ages, with children, across cultures, and even with seatmates on a plane or bus. Sometimes a person who seems quite incompatible reveals great depth, and a spiritual friendship forms despite initial dislike. We can also make kinships with authors through their writings and with the saints and mystics we are drawn to study. In contemporary congregations, mentors may work with youth preparing for baptism or confirmation—another opportunity for soulful connection. Prayer partnerships can grow into long-term spiritual bonds. When spiritual friends are separated by miles, they can mine new depths through phone calls, e-mail, and letters. Small groups that gather for prayer, spiritual sharing, or reflection offer other avenues for spiritual friendship.

A childhood love of biographies introduced me to friends of a different time and place. In the fourth grade, I watched a documentary on Helen Keller and started reading every juvenile biography of her I could find. Her spiritual strength and enthusiastic intellect shone through the pages I devoured. Florence Nightingale was another such friend made through biography, as was Laura Ingalls Wilder through her memoir-like fictional series. I felt myself joining Laura on a pioneer journey from the little house in the Big Woods to her young adulthood on the western plains. Later, as a student of mystics, I found friends who took another kind of pilgrimage, inner journeys of prayer in order to know God intimately.

Lest we be tempted to assign spiritual friendship only to private and personal realms, we should look again at the friendships Jesus cultivated during his earthly ministry. The genius of the kingdom of love that Jesus taught in the Sermon on the Mount became evident in his lived-out companionship with ordinary women and men. Jesus dined with a tax collector named Zacchaeus, heard the doubting

Thomas with patience, and conversed at a well with a woman his Jewish compatriots considered inferior. The Rabbi took time during a busy ministry simply to be with children. Knowing the value of spiritual partnership for building the kingdom of God, Jesus sent out his followers two by two. While we have no written accounts of the mutual spiritual support those pairings must have provided, we do have records from the journals of seventeenth- and eighteenth-century Quaker ministers who traveled in pairs as a matter of gospel principle. Their journals reveal the strength that these prayerful partnerships enabled. Today teachers, mission organizers, and pilgrims know the vitality that spiritual camaraderie furthers.

THE KEY INGREDIENT: LISTENING WELL

Good listening, a vital component of spiritual friendship, seems quite simple but is harder than it first appears. Before I trained as a spiritual director, I blithely reflected to my sister, a professional counselor, that her job of listening was easy. That was, until I tried it!

Quaker spiritual writer Patricia Loring asserts that prayerful listening is a challenging spiritual discipline—"to listen without agenda, without the compulsion to help, abandoning the need to appear knowledgeable, wise or comforting."[1] Such listening requires hospitality, suspending judgment, and compassion that are not achieved by effort but by letting go through contemplative prayer. Loring compares our inner process to that of a camera lens. Our inner lenses are often shut or only partially open to receive limited light. The Holy Spirit, Loring believes, invites us to "relax our grip on our defenses, on who we think we are, . . . on what is the right response."[2] By praying in and through our listening, by placing our natural prejudices before the loving scrutiny of the Spirit, we begin to truly open our hearts and hear.

It is humbling to watch the number of responses that arise in my mind when I am listening to a friend. The longer I accompany others in spiritual direction and friendship, the more I realize that I am called simply to be still. By cultivating internal stillness before God and the other, I relax the aperture to the lens of my soul; I let go of the need to find an answer or offer a wise word. This is hard work at times, for naturally I want to be useful to my friend. Nevertheless, something profound happens when one is simply being heard, metaphorically held in the spacious container that attentive silence provides.

Something profound happens when one is simply being heard.

Another dynamic that must be checked at the door in any enduring friendship is what I call the efficiency syndrome. Imagine one morning I meet with my spiritual friend over coffee, and he begins complaining about his job. It's not the first time. For months he has talked about his unfeeling boss, clients who want the job done yesterday, and his restless impulses. "Alas," I find myself inwardly sighing, "what can I offer to counter his despair?" Slowly, almost unwittingly, I begin to forsake the sacred call just to listen. I turn down the volume and turn on the automatic pilot, complete with head nods and appropriate facial gestures. My mind runs through the list of errands I have yet to do that day. *It's only practical*, I think. I realize what I am doing, but in the moment, I wonder why I need to put a lot of energy into listening. I have heard the story before. Hopefully, my friend doesn't know that I have mentally checked out.

The internal shift may not be apparent to my friend, but even kindly apathy erodes the holy edges of the container that prayerful listening enables. It's not that spiritual friendship requires perfect listening, but by applying the discipline of listening as if I were hearing for the very first time, I open space for my friend, as well as myself, to experience healing possibilities. Perhaps I as the listener will hear my friend mention a phrase or a feeling I have never heard before. Perhaps the Spirit will lead me to ask my friend a new question. As a faithful listener my primary calling is not to problem solve, to figure out the psychological reasons my friend has stayed so long in this oppressive job situation, or even to find a Bible verse with just the right message for his situation. While I may be led to offer a particular word to my friend, such leadings are rarely automatic. Prayerful attention to the other takes time. In listening with our whole hearts, we awaken to the promise of the Spirit's life-giving and transformative power for the other. We trust that the gift of prayerful presence is worth more than the advice of a well-meaning companion.

Perhaps you can remember a time when someone truly listened to you in this way and you felt the joy of finally *being heard*. You may recall the attentiveness, sense of empathy, and openness to God's mysterious nearness that your friend gave you simply by listening. I remember times when someone listened to me at this profound level of unconditional affirmation, and I felt freedom and grace. Sometimes I articulated beliefs I didn't know I held, and other times I discovered possible solutions to my problems by making new connections between seemingly disparate events. When someone heard my heart without judgment or compulsion to give a "right" answer, I have more than once been freed to hear the Spirit's voice speaking through my own words!

Such openhearted listening does not mean that the listener never suggests an idea or a resource that might benefit the other. Indeed, as we have seen, the Holy Spirit can powerfully move through the mouth of the listener. We are called to be attentive and discerning when listening just as we are in approaching a spiritual discipline like prayer. The key is more silence, less ego.

WHAT CLASSICAL SPIRITUAL FRIENDSHIP OFFERS

We have considered Christian spiritual friendship from a biblical perspective, but the term *spiritual friendship* was not actually coined until Aelred of Rievaulx, a twelfth-century abbot, wrote a book on the subject. While we will explore this beautiful text in more depth in chapter 2, it is important to briefly name this touchstone on the spiritual exercise of friendship. Aelred's book provided the first lengthy reflection on the distinctiveness of Christian friendship as compared to classical Greek notions of friendship.

Classic Greco-Roman conventions placed loyalty and virtue at the heart of authentic friendship. Faithful friends conversed about the Platonic ideals of truth, goodness, and beauty and thereby kindled a desire in the other to pursue these ideals. When two friends met for conversation or exchanged letters, they sought—as Paul did in his letters to the early church—not just to share news but also to edify the other. While taking serious account of these noble conventions in his own reflection on friendship, Aelred believed that Christian friendship was unique. It had its spiritual roots in prayer, and furthermore, Aelred pointed out, any perfection in virtuous friendship was impossible apart from Christ. Aelred observed that we humans are all too often wayward and unthinking. We react out of anger or respond to a friend out of the residue of old wounds. Our internal struggles distract us from the sacred bond of friendship. We need help—grounding of a different sort—to fulfill the spiritual vocation of friendship. Aelred felt that true friendship, like other spiritual practices of the Christian life, could only be discovered through surrender to the Spirit and obedience to Christ.

By drawing upon insights from our tradition, Christian spiritual leaders today invite us to bring this spiritual discipline into a conscious deepening of our own friendships. Indeed, when we practice spiritual disciplines like *lectio divina* (sacred reading), we relax our hold on *chronos* time (a sense of time as measured in hours and minutes) and intentionally enter *kairos* (becoming so absorbed in an activity that measures of time become secondary). We give priority, energy, and attention to these spiritual disciplines, for we recognize that very few virtuosos are born—rather, their talents are honed through practice. It is in the very donation of time to what we care about most that we find God's grace meeting us more than halfway. We discover, as Aelred said, that if we give spiritual friendship such attention, unexpected riches emerge.

In our efficiency-driven culture, the spiritual leisure to cultivate such deep friendship is hard to manage. We actually do better at justifying sports and recreation. Yet it is through cultivating sacred leisure that we are able to be fully present to one another. For most friendship pairs, setting aside a regular time to meet, perhaps once a week or once a month, is vital. However, these get-togethers no longer take place primarily in monasteries, as they did for Aelred and his brothers. Today we might find a quiet, out-of-the-way coffee shop; a river walk or greenway; a park; a kitchen after the kids have left for school; an office before the workday descends; or an unused church parlor for such appointments. The only key to location is the freedom for each person to share in an unhindered way and to pray with each other.

On one level prayer seems obvious to spiritual friendship, but praying aloud or even silently with a friend in today's culture feels vulnerable. We may fear appearing overly pious or be uncomfortable praying aloud in front of others. Habits may be ingrained even in deep friendships of many years, where the individuals might pledge prayer for each other but feel a bit embarrassed about praying aloud in the moment. Nevertheless, such a powerful act of silently or vocally opening to the Third in our midst slowly melts these inner resistances. We no longer worry about being identified as countercultural or seeming too spiritual.

WHAT SPIRITUAL FRIENDSHIP IS NOT

Spiritual friendships within the Christian community are distinguished by certain features. While similar in depth to spiritual direction, spiritual friendship is mutual. Spiritual direction, like other counseling ministries, relies on meetings between a seasoned, usually trained, spiritual guide and his or her "directee," an individual seeking support for the spiritual journey. In concord with the Holy Spirit, the spiritual director listens to the directee for an hour or so at a set appointment time, typically once a month. The spiritual hospitality of listening is offered almost solely in the direction of the directee, though directors often experience spiritual renewal through such conversations. The director supports the directee's life of prayer and experience of God, his or her spiritual practices, and the integration of these disciplines into daily life.

In contrast to spiritual direction, spiritual friends take turns sharing and listening. One of the pair may occasionally take more "air time," but in the long run balance emerges.

Friendship meetings are typically more informal than those of spiritual direction. Spiritual directors try to provide gentle detachment, which can be a gift to a directee wrestling through a dark night of the soul or confessing a sin with serious consequences for her or his immediate community. While a spiritual friend may at times offer detached wisdom, the call to mutual sharing means that she or he will in turn be called to reflect on very personal issues. It is hard to remain detached when the light shines in both directions.

Issues of power and sexuality must be considered in discerning whether a spiritual friendship is advisable.

Furthermore, because friendship usually entails other intersections in community, it's hard to keep up any kind of halo effect for long, because friends eventually see one another in all kinds of "weather." There are gifts in this difference. Layers of shared experience may enable friends to risk feelings that are blocked in more formal settings like spiritual direction. Nevertheless, since spiritual friendships often arise in a complex matrix of relationships, confidentiality must be carefully tended.

Indeed, spiritual friendship exists as one of many relationships in the Christian community. Thus, issues of power and sexuality must be considered in discerning whether a spiritual friendship is advisable. Pastors and parishioners, teachers and students, supervisors and those under them—all are involved in power relationships that hinder the mutual growth of spiritual friendship. This does not mean pastors should never open up to congregants or that teachers and students may not become good friends after graduation, but the boundaries of these roles enable their effectiveness. Like a power imbalance, the fact of our being sexual creatures must also not be ignored. Particularly as a spiritual friendship deepens, feelings of sexual attraction may arise in one or both members. While such feelings ought not be dismissed out of hand, they must be addressed consciously and prayerfully.

FOUNDATIONS OF SPIRITUAL FRIENDSHIP

Loving God

John 3:16 could have been written, "For God so befriended the world that . . ." In one parable Jesus describes God as a bridegroom who sent out servants to the streets looking for new friends to invite to the heavenly banquet (Matt. 22:1-14). Indeed, even in the face of rejection the heavenly bridegroom continues to widen the prospective pool of guests. Faithfully God befriends humankind, and God's friendship with us sustains our human friendships. God's friendship is evident in Christ's incarnation, in the amazing gift of life on this planet, and in our eternal longing to return to that first intimacy. God, our first Friend, is the grounding for all other relationships.

Simply put, human love involves attachment. Thus, if I do not nurture my primary friendship with God, I may unwittingly turn to my human friends for basic spiritual sustenance. It can be hard to lean on the everlasting arms of the sometimes hidden Divine Friend. We may miraculously hear the voice of God audibly or feel divine love carried through a breeze, but friendship with God usually requires a conscious awareness of something beyond the physical bounds of material life—an inward attention to a still, small voice.

Idolatry is typically depicted as a golden calf or, in today's world, applied to the rabid consumerism that claims our soul energies. A more subtle form of idolatry tempts us in human relationships: we want a new love to meet all our needs; we want our children to fulfill our unrealized dreams; we want our best friend to be perfectly supportive and understanding. But if we assign a false divinity to a soul friend, we undermine both the true nature of communion with the Divine and eventually the friendship itself.

Loving Self

Jesus taught that we should love our neighbors as we love ourselves, but we often fail to love the self we were given at birth. In giving us the Golden Rule, Jesus reflected a psychological truth: unless we practice compassion for our own souls, we will always struggle to truly love others. Such self-love is not the same as narcissism, a desperate search for attention that can never be satisfied. A person lacking self-compassion hops onto a treadmill of seeking adulation and devotion from others. Praise and popularity are usually short-lived, so the narcissist's wound never fully heals. There is always another performance, a new day to try to win the affection of a mate or friend or to stage a minidrama that draws emotional focus. Of course, we all need the unconditional regard of others, especially parents or care-givers, to learn how to nurture love within. And since those early foundations are rarely perfect, most of us also know the temptation to cajole others for the love we need. Nevertheless, with awareness we realize that roots of love grow as we experience the unconditional acceptance of God.

While women have traditionally been socialized into a mind-set that gives priority to the feelings of others, men also struggle to love themselves adequately. In both genders self-neglect may appear to be pious; we may inaccurately label a lack of self-regard as unselfishness. Yet we never escape our human needs, and feelings don't magically evaporate when we assume a posture of other-centeredness.

Love of self does not mean becoming self-focused and neglectful of the very neighbors that Jesus bids us love. The comparative is "as," not "more than" or "less than." Jesus calls us to a balance between self-care and awareness of the other.

A ready example can be seen in the practice of listening to one's friend. If my friendships continually put me in the role of listener and I am not listened to with some degree of equanimity, an internal disconnect may arise. One of those disconnects may be resentment. I may find myself avoiding my friend or thinking negatively about him or her. Or more subtly, I may begin to think of myself as holier or more self-sacrificing than my friend—and the tricky sin of pride finds residence in my soul. Moreover, the quality of my listening will surely suffer; I will likely become distracted by my own unspoken issues and may start projecting my own problems onto my friend. Perhaps my friend worries that the dream job she applied for will mean a salary cut, and because I have some financial woes that I have yet to face, I may project my own fears related to financial stress rather than hear the unique issues that this pay shift may mean for her. Perhaps she is being called to grow in simplicity, or perhaps she has childhood memories of a lack of money that have never been consciously addressed. Finding ways to extend care to myself enables me to care for her. With another friend or spiritual director, I may see my own unspoken worries in clear relief. I can listen anew with openhearted faithfulness to God's unique call in my friend's life.

The thirteenth-century Christian mystic Mechthild of Magdeburg describes a compelling vision. In her vision Mechthild sees herself dressed as a poor servant girl and attending a heavenly service of the Eucharist. When the Virgin Mary invites her to join the heavenly choir, Mechthild struggles with feelings of inadequacy and self-loathing. How dare she, a lowly servant, join this august body of saints in the choir? Before she can say no to Christ's mother, she looks down and finds that her dress has been transformed. She is now wearing a beautiful red-brown cloak, and a wreath of love has suddenly appeared on her head. Though she remains humble, this Cinderella transformation enables her to join the heavenly choir.

Mechthild's vision is a parable of God's deep, unconditional love for each one of us. We are loved before we can even utter the desire to be worthy. We do not earn the cloak of beauty that is wrapped around our souls or the wreath of love that God gives each of us. Divine blessing is not something we should put off through self-loathing or even benign neglect. Our childhood experiences may have wounded our self-esteem, or our Sunday school teachers may never have taught the second part of the Golden Rule. Still, the God who so loved us that Jesus was sent to incarnate that love has clothed us with unconditional regard.

Self-love can be encouraged in a variety of ways. Simple acts of mercy to oneself include adequate rest and a healthy diet, exercise, and perhaps leisure reading. Personal spiritual practices of prayer, journaling, devotional reading, and meditation foster healthy self-love, as does the experience of corporate worship. If I always volunteer for the nursery and miss regular opportunities for worship and the spiritual nurture of a good sermon, I neglect myself and may become resentful or distracted from God. By fostering my own spiritual well-being, I further the first spiritual friendship God gave me at birth—myself.

Starting from the Beginning

Before we flesh out our definition of spiritual friendship in the following chapters with biblical and historical understandings, I invite you to pause and reflect on a deep friendship in your own life. Perhaps you want to think further about your best friend in the third grade or the friend you did everything with as a teenager. Maybe you remember a teacher who took time with you and offered you space to talk through feelings. Your first soul kinship may have been formed in young adulthood—at college, in your first job, in a volunteer experience overseas. Who became your *anam cara* reflecting the truest mirror of your own soul?

Teresa of Ávila, the sixteenth-century Spanish mystic, compared times of effortless prayer to rain. And so some friendships are just given, like rain poured out from heaven as a gift to the earth. My sister, Rachel, born when I was only a year old, was given to me as a soul friend—without my asking or my effort. Of course, as siblings we had the usual squabbles, followed by quick makeups. We also competed for parental attention, and we often got each other into trouble. We automatically knew whether or not something was fair. Still, when I look back to this first and most enduring spiritual friendship of my life, I find facets in its unassuming design that translate to other true soul kinships. Two qualities in particular from this first friendship remain life-giving in the spiritual friendships I have today: *the gift of play* and *the safety to trust the other* with the priceless truth of one's soul.

Indeed Rachel and I did play! My sister and I tried on adult roles as if we were changing costumes in a multi-act drama. On Saturdays we brought our daydreams to life. We ran grocery stores, taught school, managed beauty shops, and created restaurants complete with a three-item menu (baloney sandwiches, soda, and moon pies). We directed orchestras, danced on stage as accomplished ballerinas, and went on tour as well-known singers. Rachel wrote plays that we acted. (One sounded similar to *Little Women*, which our parents were reading to us at the time.) In the safety of this primary connection, we explored the range of our souls without the limits of permanency or responsibility.

Rachel and I also giggled a lot, the kind of rippling laughter that erupts and grows stronger on a diet of restraint. In summer we ran with abandon in the warm rain, caught fireflies, and lay on our backs looking for animal shapes in the clouds. While adults must practice more reserve, the play of hearts and minds ought not to be foreign to their friendships either. Soul-knitting experiences of laughter and tears inhabit relationships of the Spirit.

Even as the particulars of friendships change with age, the ability to play remains vital. Adults may play with language, share daydreams of vocation, or bring the wonder of childhood into the present. A couple of years ago I went walking with a spiritual friend in the natural area behind the campus where we teach. As we ambled along, my friend suddenly stopped me, motioning me to be quiet. "Watch the frogs," he whispered. One by one, two by two, frogs leapt into the pond as if by signal to the vibration of our footfalls. I could only laugh at the sight. The safety of our kinship gave us room to giggle, to encounter creation playfully. Through such encounters in friendship, we may again touch the sure familiarity of God's hand. We might remember, beyond words or images, the heaven we came from, before all of the seriousness of living set in.

The second quality integral to friendship—spaciousness for the soul to speak freely—was another gift of my sister's friendship. Rachel and I shared the same bedroom until we went to high school. From our respective twin beds, we followed a nightly ritual of talking until one of us dozed off; the next day we usually did not remember who went to sleep first. Though unschooled in the classical spiritual practice of examen, we were in fact doing just that, regularly reviewing our days together. Mom and Dad typically used a two- or three-warning system to get us to hush. The first warning was clear but gentle: "Time to settle down, girls." So we'd quiet down, listen for the footsteps to fade, and then one of us would follow the impulse to share another story, experience, or feeling. The second warning would come in louder and firmer tones: "This is it, girls! No more talking." Based on our reading of the parental seriousness meter, we might turn over to pillows and dreams, or we might risk, in even softer voices, that one remaining story that couldn't wait until morning to be told.

As adults we know that authentic friendship is found with someone who accepts us as we are. A sure sign of spiritual friendship is when we feel willingness, even a desire, to risk disclosing our true self. Stressful transitions, times of profound grief and loss, moments when we must release some anxiety or fear, hopes we long to express that cannot yet be voiced in public—these are the moments when nothing is as comforting as a companion with whom we can be completely transparent.

A sure sign of spiritual friendship is when we feel willingness, even a desire, to risk disclosing our true self.

During my senior year of college I did a stint as a student teacher in a first-grade classroom. I had settled rightly on my life's work of teaching, but I not yet found the right age group. At school on good days I was bored and restless; on bad days I felt like a failure. I worried that I had missed my calling altogether. Rachel was no longer in the next bed or down the hall; she lived in another dormitory. One particularly awful day I left the elementary school in tears and found my way to her door. I had other friends by then, but I needed the certainty of my sister's unquestioning acceptance. She could hear the tears of my heart and intuitively knew the right ways to spark my own rediscovery of hope for the future.

The consciousness to name Christ as the one who knit our friendship formed gradually for Rachel and me. I picture in my mind's eye the gentle spirit of Christ hovering between our beds, smiling at two little girls staring at the ceiling with sparkling eyes. Natural wonderings about God and Jesus arose between us without pretense. Family prayers, stories of Jesus, and hymns extended as a backdrop to our play, our nightly chats, and the nascent spiritual life we were individually claiming.

CHAPTER 2

Gifts from the Tradition

Growing up Protestant, I did not have much awareness of our Catholic forebears. In college I took the requisite humanities courses and memorized watershed dates in the history of Christianity, but I had yet to really count the first fifteen centuries before the Protestant Reformation as part of my own story. Not until I studied church history in seminary did I taste the joys of our common heritage. There I learned that my Catholic roots were not extraneous, nor the centuries irrelevant. In particular I became excited by the rich history of women mystics who were also beloved saints of the church. I awakened to the incredible legacy that monasticism gave to Christian prayer and spiritual formation.

In this chapter we will explore some of the roots of Christian friendship that have been tended by our friends within the Roman Catholic Church, reexamining the monastic roots of spiritual friendship. We will also look at the rich legacy of the communion of saints as another way that spiritual friendship may touch us.

Aelred of Rievaulx and the Vocation of Spiritual Friendship

Aelred of Rievaulx (1110–67 CE) was born in a time of religious and social upheaval in England. As a young man he enjoyed the high life of serving in the Scottish royal court, but soon sparks from the spiritual awakening of the twelfth century reached his soul. Men and women newly ablaze with the love of God sought to live out their conversion through monastic vocation. Aelred answered the call of Christ by choosing to enter one of the strictest monastic orders, the Cistercians. His spiritual growth must have been rapid, for in a relatively short time he was elected abbot. Aelred's sermons and writings demonstrated a spiritual authority graced by quiet humility. His treatise on spiritual friendship—written in the dialogical style of his Roman predecessor, Cicero—described the vocation of friendship as one of the highest Christian spiritual disciplines.

> Aelred described the vocation of friendship as one of the highest Christian spiritual disciplines.

Unlike the hierarchical medieval conventions for marriage, friendship provided potential for equality and mutuality. Beyond his in-depth reading of Cicero on the virtues of friendship, Aelred saw analogies between spiritual friendship and monastic life. Saint Benedict's rule identified equality and hospitality as key to the right ordering of religious community, virtues also critical to good friendship. Even as an abbot, Aelred understood his role to be one of service to his brothers, being a guide to the community rather than its master. The monastic spirit of hospitality also permeated Aelred's vision of Christian friendship. With reverential kindness monks were to welcome travelers and strangers alike as long-lost friends—as if each one might be the Christ. Daily life in the monastery drew upon the Christian virtues of humility, kindness, patience, and fidelity, qualities needed as well in long-term friendships. Although he regretted the immature quality of his youthful alliances, Aelred gleaned insights from those early relationships. In his book Aelred contrasted their lack of depth with more mature kinships built on the classical virtues of friendship and rooted spiritually in Christ.

In his short but meaty text Aelred describes the degrees of friendship. Friendship flows naturally from human desires for companionship and affection as well as a longing for goodness. Friendship blooms wherever people work and play together, and some of these relationships grow on a spiritual level. A spiritual friendship may emerge when "a similarity in life, morals, and pursuits" is evident and each person desires to conform life to the will of God, a way of justice and compassion.[1] In a spiritual friendship, Aelred asserts, one's basic security no longer resides in the ways of friendship itself (shared interests, humor, and affection) but is increasingly grounded in each friend's loyalty to Christ. "Here we are, you and I, and I hope a third, Christ, is in our midst," writes Aelred. "For what more sublime can be said of friendship, what more true, what more profitable, than that it ought to, and is proved to, begin in Christ, continue in Christ, and be perfected in Christ?"[2]

The similarity of life, morals, and pursuits to which Aelred referred is a compatibility deeper than lifestyle or disposition. Spiritual friends grow their relationship roots in a soil that is "holy, voluntary, and true."[3] By using the word *holy*, Aelred was not introducing a superhuman level of goodness; rather, he was talking about the desire to look to Christ as the mentor, guide, and source for such friendships. The word *true* reflects the eternal nature of an authentic spiritual friendship. If a friendship dies because of betrayal, insult, or distrust, it must have—in Aelred's mind—already lacked a firm grounding in Christ.

We may take for granted the voluntary quality of friendship. We choose our friends freely. But if we look closely at our own motives and those of others in making friends, we may recognize something other than soul spontaneity. When a thought or feeling is voluntary, it arises naturally without external designs or constraints. Quakers describe this motion as a "leading"—the guidance of the Holy Spirit in one's soul. On the other hand, if we instead decide to become someone's "friend" because knowing him or her will heighten our status or further our own aims, we have manipulated the voluntary nature of that soul connection.

According to Aelred, true spiritual friendship requires emotional honesty and integrity.

We may think that this would not happen in Christian friendships, where agape love is foundational. Sadly, though, even in the church we see political scheming at work in the formation of friendships, small groups, and community. A church can end up with cliques, where hidden rules justify one's place in the inner circle. At its best the church seeks to follow Christ's injunction of welcoming the "least of these" as if they were the greatest. Applying this gospel virtue to spiritual friendship, Aelred invites us to test our motives. Are we forming friendships freely, without applying secret conditions?

True spiritual friendship, according to Aelred, requires emotional honesty and integrity. A contrast clarifies his point. When salespeople and politicians wield friendship's charms to persuade us to a particular end—whether it is to buy a certain car or adopt a certain political stance—we feel uncomfortable. Such smiling persuasion leaves a bad taste in our mouths, even when it leads to something we believe to be good. Instead, notes Aelred, if a true friend wants to influence his or her companion, the persuasion is done purely for the sake of love: love of God and love of the friend.

Love and justice are the two pillars of relationships in Christ. Thus, true spiritual friendship cannot be developed through alliances whose purpose is to stir up prejudice or ill feeling, or even—Aelred would contend—should they be based on milder deceptions. If he were to look in on our contemporary relationships, Aelred would invite us to carefully tend our integrity, not to remake ourselves for the sake of peer approval, for example.

If we are honest with ourselves, we know our human motives are typically mixed. The following is a possible scenario where the subtlety of motives complicates authentic friendship. Suppose I have recently befriended a homeless single mother at a local soup kitchen, offering her a listening ear as she shares her struggles to find a suitable apartment for herself and her young child. Empathy and genuine care arise in my heart, and I sense deep joy as we brainstorm possible avenues for her. Signs of a soulful kinship begin to grow, and we arrange to get together again.

Driving home, I celebrate with God the gift of this connection, but then I begin to think about my own goodness, about my faithfulness to God in reaching out to the "less fortunate." In addition to the pride that such self-congratulation engenders, I slowly but surely begin putting distance between myself and my new friend. I forget that I too could be a homeless mother. I start counting the stars in my crown rather than responding openly to the love that arose spontaneously in our community of two. Even more subtly, I may begin to think that because I have more material resources, I have more to offer the friendship than she does.

Just as Jesus decried the Pharisees' and Sadducees' leaven of religious superiority, so Aelred would caution us to watch the leaven of pride or partiality that can infect our friendships, keeping them from becoming mutual and appropriately vulnerable to Christ at work in the heart. Aelred expands on this point, offering the biblical illustration of Jonathan, who esteemed his friendship with the shepherd David more than his royal lineage:

> Therefore, in friendship, which is the perfect gift of nature and grace alike, let the lofty descend, the lowly ascend; the rich be in want, the poor become rich; and thus let each communicate his condition to the other, so that equality may be the result. . . . [I]f you chance to find yourself the superior in those things which we have mentioned, then do not hesitate to abase yourself before your friend, to give him your confidence, to praise him if he is shy, and to confer honor upon him in inverse proportion to that warranted by his lowliness and poverty. Jonathan, that excellent youth, paying no heed to a royal crown or to the hope of regal power, entered upon a covenant with David. He made the servant, David, an equal in friendship in the Lord.[4]

While we cannot ignore factors of power and position in friendship, as we will explore in chapter 6, we can still witness Christ's friendship with us as self-emptying for the sake of love.

Aelred also believed that true spiritual friendship would pass a test of four qualities: loyalty, right intention, discretion, and patience. Loyalty is tested by time and adversity; the loyal friend sees the heart of his or her friend and does not count the cost of hard times. A loyal friend guards the well-being of a companion with fierce compassion. Loyalty, notes Aelred, also calls upon each friend to maintain confidentiality.

Aelred might compare right intention to Jesus' use of "pure in heart" in the sixth beatitude: I love God not for what God can do for me but because God is the One I love and worship. Likewise, I am called to love my friend with unconditional regard, relying on grace rather than measuring what I might get out of the friendship.

In the test of discretion Aelred invites us to pause and look at the character of the person to whom our hearts are quickly drawn. Is this new friend kind to you but thoughtless toward others? Does he or she lack wisdom or the ability to learn from circumstances? Aelred cautions us to discern the integrity of the new friend's words and actions.

Aelred believed true spiritual friendship would pass a test of four qualities:

1. Loyalty

2. Right intention

3. Discretion

4. Patience

Finally, Aelred asks, is a patient character evident on both sides of the friendship? Human friendship will naturally involve failure on someone's part, perhaps a careless breach of confidence or an unkind comment. Aelred reminds us that patience is vital to enduring friendship: to clear up misunderstandings, to seek reconciliation, and to forgive the other as Christ forgives. At times a good friend may also need to speak a hard truth to us in love; we, applying patience, are called to receive this word without losing heart.

Although Aelred held up high standards for spiritual friendship, he was quick to balance these moral ideals with the joy and delight that soul kinship brings. Where else but with a good friend can we be ourselves, relieve our doubts and fears, and receive encouragement for the journey? It is therefore psychologically beneficial that we choose our soul companions on life's journey wisely so that we have safe, loving, and prayerful kinships to look at our heart's depths. Aelred wrote that spiritual friendship is eternal, so the care we give to such friendships now will reap enduring growth for us and for the other. Aelred esteemed spiritual friendship so highly that he saw analogies in friendship that sound similar to those describing marriage today. Through Christ, Aelred believed, friends might eventually grow one heart, one soul.

Exemplars of Christian Friendship:
Francis and Clare

Although they probably didn't know about Aelred's book on Christian friendship, Francis of Assisi (1181–1226) and Clare of Assisi (1194–1253) lived out Aelred's vision of spiritual friendship. To explore their friendship, we need to recall the story of Saint Francis and the sometimes forgotten Saint Clare.

Popular images of Saint Francis—such as the statues that adorn our gardens—portray a peaceful, almost passive figure, but the Francis of history, while humble, was hardly meek and mild. Before his conversion he was the exuberant playboy of Assisi. One day in a dramatic gesture, the youthful Francis signed up to be a knight. He didn't last long on the battlefield; he was taken prisoner and returned home a year later a changed person. After his time away, he viewed his comfortable world as a well-to-do cloth merchant's son differently. Francis saw the sharp inequities between rich and poor and, to his father's dismay, began reaching out to the most feared of the city, the lepers. The church, with its wealth and status, now seemed alien to him. Stopping to pray at a broken-down chapel outside of Assisi, Francis heard a voice calling him out into mission. Francis vowed to follow in Christ's footsteps, and this would soon mean embracing a life of poverty, itinerant preaching, and unknown to him at the time, founding a simple religious community like the one shared by Jesus and his disciples.

Francis embodied a charisma of joy, befriending all of creation as part of his friendship with God. He was known to stop at a field and talk to the birds, calling them his dear little brothers. He reminded them to praise God, who provided them with food, which, as Jesus said in the Gospel of Matthew, they had neither sown nor reaped. Although Francis knew hunger and cold firsthand, as well as social ridicule, he held fast to the ecstasy of God's love that fills creation. He seemed fearless in his desire to live as Jesus lived, preaching the gospel on every street corner. Francis even went on mission to share the gospel with the sultan in Egypt. Amazingly, though it was the time of the fifth Crusade, the Islamic ruler received Francis's friendly overture peacefully. Francis's evenhanded, compassionate befriending of the poor and the sick, of neighbor and so-called enemy alike, and of animate and inanimate creation epitomized the virtue of right intention that Aelred elevated.

Born into even greater privilege than Francis was the younger Clare. Destined to marry into nobility, she also made an amazing conversion. As a teen Clare heard Francis preaching at the church in Assisi and—properly chaperoned—met with him for spiritual direction. Clare later boldly escaped her home at age eighteen to join Francis and his band of brothers in a radical pursuit of the way of Jesus. In an act of surrender to Christ, she asked Francis to cut her long hair, which also symbolized her rejection of marriage.

The first woman to join Francis, she initially remained secluded in a Benedictine convent until a house adjoining the chapel of San Damiano—where Francis had heard the voice of Christ—could be prepared. While unable to join Francis in itinerancy, Clare nevertheless adopted a cloistered life of prayer, hospitality, simplicity, and poverty in loyal companionship to her brother in Christ. Soon other women joined her, and after Francis's death Clare finally was able to secure the pope's approval for her order and her monastic rule, the first one written by a woman.

While Francis's extroverted ways of befriending were popularly known, the enclosed Clare was more quietly known by her sisters to be generous and kind. Although she was their abbess, Clare took the least, be it food or clothing. When sisters returned from errands in town, she washed and kissed their feet. If Clare saw a sister struggling with a temptation or problem, she secretly called the sister aside, sat with her, and offered her own tears as consolation. Tenderness abounds in letters that Clare wrote to Agnes, a young woman in Prague who was moved by Franciscan spirituality and entered into prayerful seclusion in the way of Clare. "O mother and daughter, spouse of the King of all ages," Clare wrote to Agnes, "if I have not written to you as often as your soul and mine as well desire and long for, do not wonder or think that the fire of love for you glows less sweetly."[5] Clare's humble and gentle approach to her daughters of faith reflected the patience Aelred believed to be central to spiritual friendship.

In the friendship story of Francis and Clare, we see glimmers of the courtly love tradition, such as rituals of courtesy and unwavering devotion. Still, the chastity of this loving friendship was not questioned. Their friendship embraced at its center loyal love for Christ, mutual contentment in a lifestyle of gospel simplicity, tender charity toward all, and an effervescent praise of God and creation. Francis was reluctant to spend much time in person with Clare—out of concern for propriety—but stories of their encounters reveal deep mutual esteem. In one account, Francis and some of his brothers met Clare and a couple of her sisters for a simple meal. The meal was not touched before the dinner guests were joyfully swept up into an ecstatic, mystical state, and a local crowd came rushing to see the source of the fiery glow. Perhaps like the biblical witnesses at Pentecost who saw tongues of fire over the disciples, the light seen around Francis and Clare gave evidence of hearts united mystically in the love of God.[6]

In a day when passion is equated with sexual expression, the nature of the relationship between Francis and Clare may seem unfulfilling. Yet their friendship, like that of Francis de Sales and Jane de Chantal four centuries later in seventeenth-century France, reveals the beauty of chaste soul kinships between male and female as well as between gay friends. Spiritual friendship may offer a spaciousness that is difficult to maintain in the daily negotiations of a committed love relationship. Of course, some friendships involve risk because of an undercurrent of sexual feeling, but with care and honesty such friendships can flourish. An application of Aelred's tests of spiritual friendship may help. Some questions to consider might include these:

- Will I remain loyal to the gift of soul connection with my friend, as well as to the commitments we each have, without acting on the impulse of sexual desire?

- Will I enjoy the loving regard I have for my friend without trying to get sexual benefit from him or her?

- Will I carefully consider my own self-care around sexuality so I am not blindsided by unfulfilled longings?

I have appreciated both the men and the women in my life with whom friendship has deepened to a spiritual level. In these friendships, issues of romantic feeling, if they arose, were addressed thoughtfully. The above questions proved helpful in dealing with such situations.

In relationships where conflicting emotions or sexual feelings persist, you may need to consult a spiritual director or a therapist. Perhaps you have neglected self-care, or the feelings may suggest a deepening love relationship with God that seeks expression. Wise counsel, prayer, and at times an open discussion with the friend in question are ways to safeguard the relationship.

The Gift of the Communion of Saints

It was March 1994. Forsythia was blooming, and baby green fuzz had softened the dark gray lines of winter. With a book under my arm, intending to gather data for a paper for my seminary class, I headed for a quiet coffee shop in Richmond, Virginia's West End. The book I carried would become one of the most important readings of my life; it was *Evelyn Underhill: Artist of the Infinite Life*, a biography of the British spiritual writer.

Along with my coffee, I drank in the story of Underhill, a mystics scholar and spiritual director at the turn of the twentieth century. In late Victorian England, Underhill's spiritual calling put her at odds with the traditional roles for women of her generation. I read how she had spiritual openings as a teen and searched earnestly as a young woman, how she studied the mystics of the church and found her way to a deeper experience of Christ. Her life wove together vocations of prayer, writing, retreat leading, and spiritual direction. My mind raced almost breathlessly through the pages, for I felt as though I had met someone who understood my own strange calling. Pulling my chair up close to the fire of an imagined English drawing room, I listened as Underhill's heart spoke to mine. I felt God's love in a profound confirmation of my very being and vocation. And I knew experientially the glowing fire of the communion of saints.

Spiritual friendship need not be limited to time and space dimensions; there remains an eternal aspect to the meeting of kindred souls. The writer to the Hebrews knew this. "Therefore, since we are surrounded by so great a cloud of witnesses, let us also lay aside every weight and the sin that clings so closely, and let us run with perseverance the race that is set before us, looking to Jesus the pioneer and perfecter of our faith" (Heb. 12:1-2). It is no wonder that centuries later we return to familiar Bible stories. We garner moral courage from the image of Daniel bravely facing a den of hungry lions. We sit expectantly with a teenage Mary in the glow of angelic light, listening

We can draw strength from a cloud of witnesses who lived long after New Testament dust settled: women and men who encountered the living Christ in their own times.

with her to an amazing prophecy. We contemplate the true meaning of joy in Paul, who, writing to the Philippians, extols the benefit of imprisonment so the gospel can spread. The narratives of their lives and their testimonies of divine-human encounter strengthen us for a race in a very different time and place.

Likewise, we can draw strength from a cloud of witnesses who lived long after New Testament dust settled: women and men who encountered the living Christ in their own times. As a seminary student—and relatively ignorant of the many shoulders I was standing on—my study of church history was somewhat like meeting dozens of new friends. In particular, a light went on in my soul when I encountered women mystics from the medieval period.

For most of my adolescence and young adulthood, my romantic spirituality had made me feel a bit like an odd-ball. I often sang along to love songs on the radio, directing them to God. I felt that there could be no higher expression for devotion to God than romantic love. In seminary I realized that my spirituality was not so strange after all. I met women of history whose passion for Christ was nourished by the Song of Solomon, who found images and metaphors in the fires of romance that expressed their longing for God. Here as well were women emboldened by God in the midst of a patriarchal church, writing down their visions with the authority of God's confirmation within. I learned about Mechthild of Magdeburg, whose desire for God was so strong that at age twenty she left home to devote her entire being to prayer. She joined the Beguine movement, a lay movement responsible for some of the earliest hospices. I also met the headstrong Teresa of Ávila. Her ardor for God led her into lifelong mystical adventure and energized her for strenuous travels in her fifties and sixties to reform her monastic order. Then I discovered Julian of Norwich, whose theology of God was permeated by images of tender parenthood, whose vision and experience of Christ's suffering gave her such confidence that in the midst of the darkest days of the bubonic plague she could say with deep assurance that "all shall be well."

These medieval soul companions came alive to me through their writings as they shared their visions and insights about God's unique encounter with every soul. Unlike the stories of women in scripture that were told by others, these women wrote about their own experiences and described the everyday struggles they faced. They shared their dry times in prayer as well as feelings of inadequacy about how to articulate their mystical encounters with God. They also voiced their enduring prayer that the church might finally live out the kingdom vision of Jesus. My new "friends" of the Spirit cheered me on, reminding me that I was part of a larger circle of women called to nurture others in the spiritual life.

I have also come to count Spirit-filled companions of recent history, like my mentor Evelyn Underhill, among my spiritual friends. One of those is Oscar Romero, the archbishop of El Salvador, who was gunned down in 1980 for bringing to light the military oppression of his people. While attending a service honoring his feast day at a local Catholic church several years ago, I was moved by the power of his story: a church leader who had once turned a blind eye to political realities transformed into a prophet defending the "least of these." Once his ministry had been revolutionized by the Spirit, he ended up with only three years to live. During those few years he used his power in countless ways—weekly radio sermons, boycotts, public demonstrations—to bring hope to the peasants he served. At this quiet, candlelit service I opened up my Protestant heart to the grace and mystery of reverence for the saints. I realized that the saints remind us that Christ's incarnation continues in a myriad of ways when we ordinary humans say yes to God's word within. Today Oscar Romero continues to prod me with the question: Am I furthering the kingdom of God or propping up the status quo through my choices and actions? This question makes me squirm, but then, good friends are known to do that.

The communion of saints is not limited to those with feast days named in their honor. It includes all who have died in Christ. No doubt you can think of family, friends, teachers, and mentors who have passed to the other side—and yet their memory and even presence are palpable. Though my aunt Betty died almost twenty years ago, she is one of those who sit in my "balcony." She showed others the way of love by example. In midlife Betty and her husband adopted a little boy who turned out to be severely mentally disabled. He was cherished, living at home until his late teens. Betty was also a math professor who often stayed late to tutor students who were struggling in her courses. I learned more about compassion from her than from any sermon or youth talk.

One summer in our adolescence Rachel and I took a four-hour bus trip to stay with my aunt and her family for a week. Right away we noticed that the neighborhood kids congregated almost daily at her house. I was mystified as to why they came, but then I began to see that it was because Aunt Betty took sincere interest in each one. She listened and encouraged. For many of these latchkey kids, she was an unofficial summer camp counselor.

Almost everything went well during Rachel's and my visit, except that I disliked one of the neighborhood girls; she was bossy and always wanted her way. At night I complained to Rachel, never thinking my aunt would overhear. If she did, she didn't let on. One morning over breakfast Aunt Betty simply told us the sad tale of the girl's family life. She never spoke to me directly about my grumblings, but inwardly I saw my judgment in stark relief. Aunt Betty moved me to see this girl with new eyes, and her lesson in compassion left an indelible imprint on my soul. In subsequent visits I found myself watching Aunt Betty to see how she cared about others. Years after her death, I still encounter Aunt Betty in my dreams; in times of crisis I imagine talking with her. Finally, as I have become an aunt myself, her ongoing spiritual kinship informs how I love and guide my own nephews.

As you reflect on the passage from Hebrews 12 and the spiritual lineage in your own family, consider who has been in your "balcony," cheering you on in your spiritual life. Who in the present and from your past has confirmed what is deepest in you? What have you learned from these persons, and what are they still teaching you?

Is there some historical figure you have felt drawn to but don't know much about? Perhaps you would like to get acquainted with a saint, a mystic, a missionary, or some other spiritual leader through the pages of a biography, book of this person's writings, or even a video. You may find that as you learn more about him or her, you strike a kinship across time and gain new inspiration for the life of faith.

CHAPTER 3

Ruth and Naomi:
Loyal Love

Men as well as women know the ache for someone with whom to share their deepest thoughts and feelings, hopes and disappointments. In the book of Ruth we find an incredible story of an unusual spiritual friendship.

AN UNEXPECTED KINSHIP

Naomi and Ruth were not sisters, nor were they related as mother and daughter. With the death of Naomi's son, the obligations of blood ties no longer bound them to each other. Hebrew hearers of this story generations ago would have been struck by the strangeness of this alliance of in-laws. Furthermore, Naomi and Ruth not only differed in terms of their place in the family system, but also in age, culture, and religious tradition. Nonetheless, these two traveled together, made a home, and helped each other survive through desperate times. They did so with a sense of *hesed*, or covenantal love, and some remarkable chutzpah. Because of their devotion to each other, generations have remembered them for the fruit borne of such loyal love.

53

Ruth is a practical book concerned with property issues. The canon reserved a place for it primarily because it delineates the ancestry of David. Typically, when the book of Ruth is theologically mined, interpreters reflect on the symbolic power of the story: a foreigner finds a place in the overarching narrative of the Hebrew scriptures—a story with ramifications for inclusivity not unlike the Gospel parable of the good Samaritan. Setting aside this theological issue for now, we can focus on the wisdom this story teaches about enduring friendship. What does the story say about being called into the vocation of friendship? How is covenantal love vital to spiritual friendship? How can a friend help another discern life-changing decisions? What might the fruit of a friendship look like? What role do shared projects play in the vocation of spiritual friendship?

As you reflect on Ruth and Naomi's story, I invite you to remember persons who have walked down life's meandering paths and uneven pavement with you. Remember too some of the uncommon friendships that mattered on your journey. Perhaps you call to mind an elderly coworker who became dear to you or a neighbor very unlike you in temperament or political persuasion whom you now count as a family member. As you read this chapter, think about those who have walked with you through dark nights of the soul, who trusted God for you when you struggled to believe. Maybe some of the friendships you recall will be as rare as the one between these two very different women who traveled the "road of shards" together.[1] Such surprising friendships, the story suggests, can heal more than personal wounds; they may even heal the rifts that divide culture, denominations, gender, and life experience.

CALLED INTO A COVENANT OF FRIENDSHIP

And so we recall the story of Ruth. The book opens with a famine in Judah, which leads Elimelech and his wife, Naomi, to take their two sons to Moab to find food. After Elimelech dies there, Naomi decides to remain with her two sons, who marry Moabite women, Orpah and Ruth. Ten years later both of her sons die, leaving her in a foreign country without male relatives. Since widows of that time had no means of sustenance unless they relied on their benefactors—their closest male relatives—a bereft Naomi probably realized that she would have a better chance of survival if she returned to Judah, where harvests abounded once again. As we might imagine, by now the layers of grief had most likely made her homesickness unbearable. So Naomi decides to return home, and her daughters-in-law beg to go with her. Naomi tries to dissuade them, reminding them that they will have a better opportunity to remarry if they stay in Moab. Orpah recognizes her mother-in-law's wisdom, but Ruth remains steadfast; she will go with Naomi nonetheless.

The benevolent relationship among Naomi, Ruth, and Orpah is remarkable in and of itself, for it was forged despite—or perhaps through—the trauma of great loss: death and childlessness. Indeed, there could have been emotional distance among the three women. Naomi could have in part blamed Orpah and Ruth for her destitution in a foreign land. After all, where were grandsons to care for her in old age? Orpah and Ruth might have turned away from the ever-present reminder of their lost husbands etched in their mother-in-law's face and the seeming betrayal of her Hebrew God. Instead, their desire to go with Naomi speaks of something deep and good among all three. When Orpah decides to follow Naomi's advice and return to her people, it is a sad parting.

The unexpected twist is not Orpah's return, which makes good sense, but rather Ruth's amazing decision, a discernment of will and spirit that is foolish by all accounts. If it were an oath made by a love-struck teenage girl to a James Dean–looking guy on a motorcycle, we might understand the feeling. But there is no music playing in the background as two lovebirds ride off into the sunset. Or if this were an oath made out of loyalty to religion or country, we might recognize the conviction. However, Ruth's covenant to Naomi counters both of these typical loyalties.

The most familiar passage in the book of Ruth is one often recited at weddings. As a teen, I was disappointed to learn that these romantic verses were actually spoken by a young woman to her mother-in-law! But now Ruth's pledge to Naomi has become a source of inspiration to me about the potential of friendship love. There is unexpected beauty in this solemn vow offered by one widow to another, hoping to convince the other that she might be her companion through "thick and thin." Against Naomi's convincing case for returning to Moab, Ruth declares,

> Don't urge me to leave you or to turn back from you.
> Where you go I will go, and where you stay, I will stay.
> Your people will be my people and your God my God.
> Where you die I will die, and there will I be buried.
> (Ruth 1:16-17, NIV)

Naomi is quiet but finally seems persuaded to accept her daughter-in-law's devotion. Naomi has witnessed daring courage in her young friend's devotion.

In fact, although it may not be expressed so dramatically, courage is an essential foundation for any abiding spiritual friendship. Certainly, Ruth has courage, but so does Naomi. Here is an elderly widow with two daughters-in-law, both of whom are crying to go with her. Naomi could have thought, *It's true, I am all alone and could really use the help of these two young women. They could probably do some gleaning to help us survive. If only for the journey itself, there would be safety in numbers.* Yet Naomi draws upon a deeper part of herself—a reserve of spiritual strength—and speaks the truth to her young relatives. "You are risking too much here. I care too much about you to let you come with me. I want you to stay where you will have a chance to marry and have a family. Look, let's be practical. Even if I were able to conceive tonight, you couldn't wait for these boys to grow up." No, brave Naomi is willing to go it alone. She has been faithful to Aelred's conviction that a true friend persuades the other toward only the most loving of directions.

Courage is an essential foundation for any abiding spiritual friendship.

Ruth displays courage in the vow she offers. For the sake of her love and loyalty to Naomi, Ruth risks cultural familiarity and the chance for remarriage. She becomes willing to swim upstream for the rest of her life, to cast her lot with another widow eking out a hard existence. And she is willing to embrace a foreign faith. What if the Moabite god Chemosh followed her to the border of Judah, striking her with a bolt of lightning as she crossed the border to serve the alien god? Still, Ruth resolutely declares to her mother-in-law, "Here's my life; I give it to you." In her vow we hear intimations of her descendant Jesus, who essentially said to his friends, "I am willing to lay down my life for you."

Ruth's promise is one of the clearest declarations of *hesed* love in all of scripture. The Hebrew *hesed* is a particular love; it is the enduring, steadfast love of God, a compassion that never wanes. Joyfully the author of Lamentations declares, "Every morning God's mercy is new again" (Lam. 3:22-23, paraphrased). God makes this vow of unceasing love to each one of us.

Ruth's pledge of *hesed* would have been dramatic for the Hebrew reader, just as Jesus' parable of the Samaritan offering *hesed* to the one left for dead would later surprise his audience. In the Old Testament story another outsider—a Moabite no less—offers God's covenantal love to the Jew, Naomi. Moreover, as Aelred noted about the nature of true friendship, *hesed* does not seek a return on its investment. Ruth offers her vow to Naomi with no foresight of the happy conclusion we can easily flip to at the end of the fourth chapter.

Ruth's promise to Naomi is one of the clearest declarations of hesed love—the enduring, steadfast love of God—in all of scripture.

Where do we see this kind of courage in spiritual friendship? Usually a spiritual friendship doesn't demand that we leave our homeland or wrestle with choices about our very survival. No, in our day we more often just say good-bye to dear friends, with earnest pledges of e-mail and visits. Yet there are those moments in spiritual friendship—and they happen repeatedly—when we are called to be vulnerable and to speak courageously. Inside we feel a fear, a rumbling. *Well, maybe I don't need to say this now. Perhaps I could wait for a better time.* But the stirring within us bids us to speak in this moment.

Courage is also needed at friendship junctures. You may feel called to deepen a friendship when the ostensible reason for the friendship is gone. The art class you were taking together is over; you are no longer working on the same Habitat for Humanity project; your walking buddy has moved to another state. Taking a deep breath, you go to this friend and share your hope for a future. "I really would like to go further on this journey with you." Though not as precarious as the risk Ruth took, you risk rejection or not being taken seriously. The friend may respond, "Sure, let's get together next week," but next week never comes.

Risk is also involved in sharing with a friend something that we have only told God. Ruth exposes the longings of her heart to Naomi, and instinctively, we recognize Ruth's vulnerability. It is scary to share secrets deeply held in the heart, be they declarations of great feeling or—by contrast—confessions of a grievous sin that still troubles. Yet we know that risking this tender part of ourselves, especially if we are really heard in love, can allow a relieving grace to wash over us.

Perhaps one reason couples borrow Ruth's oath as inspiration for weddings is that it expresses the eternal paradox of love: the intertwinement of risk and covenant. I decide to risk because I trust your love for me to remain steadfast. Your love for me deepens and becomes more steadfast as I risk more of myself. And so goes the intricate weaving of loyal love. We know the depth of Ruth's covenant love for Naomi because in her vow she clearly names the risks: never seeing her home again (there were no flights between Judah and Moab!), stepping outside of her language and culture, and converting to a God she only learned to trust through Naomi. We hear reverberations of Abraham's risk of homeland and kinship to follow God's voice, and we remember the covenant God made with him.

Over time, that dance of vulnerability and unwavering fidelity creates the foundation for true spiritual friendship.

One of my friends offers such *hesed* love to me. In the almost twenty years of our spiritual friendship, I have never known her to reject anything I have told her. Because we are good friends, I have also heard her pain in the back-and-forth flow of friendship; this too helps me to risk. In my mind's eye, her face has become an image of grace for me. When she offers her gentle smile and her eyes are filled with empathy, I experience the embodiment of God's compassion for me.

The Wisdom of a Discerning Heart

Another gift of an enduring spiritual friendship is the wisdom gleaned from regular discernment. Returning to the story of Ruth and Naomi, we now find the two friends living passably in Judah. Ruth is gleaning at the field of a relative of Naomi's husband. The relative, Boaz, sees Ruth and kindly offers her protection against possible untoward advances by the workers. He also commends her character, noting the sacrifice she has made in leaving her native land. Boaz blesses her, "May you have a full reward from the LORD, the God of Israel, under whose wings you have come for refuge!" (Ruth 2:12). Although he offers her a meal and directs his servants to do other good things for her, Boaz doesn't act on his regard for her in terms we're familiar with. At the beginning of the third chapter, Naomi knows it is time to speak up! And so we read Naomi's thoughtful words of discernment to Ruth, where she directs her daughter-in-law in a cultural practice designed to show romantic intention toward Boaz.

Indeed, loyal spiritual friends prove invaluable in the prayerful work of discernment. Because as friends we accompany each other over time, we can help each other name what the heart is saying, how God may be leading.

However, as we reflected earlier about good listening skills, friends should be cautious when it comes to giving advice. Like Naomi, we should wait for the right time and the leading to speak.

Unlike Naomi, though, spiritual friends today have many other discernment tools to draw from in the Christian heritage. One tool is the Ignatian practice of examen. Examen is a spiritual practice for paying attention to the Holy Spirit's movements in our daily lives; it may be used individually in a private review of the day, week, month, or longer season. Friends may share this practice on retreat or in small groups or as part of a friendship ritual already in place, like a weekly routine of walking. More in-depth examens between friends may be applied when discerning problems big and small, such as vocational direction, the next step in responding to a difficult teenager, or in deciding whether to volunteer for a particular church committee. By listening for what Ignatius of Loyola called the "consolations" and "desolations" between and amidst the words of a pondering friend, we can help her or him to hear what the soul may be saying beneath the pros and cons.

"Consolations" refer to feelings that bring a sense of freedom, peace, acceptance, and joy. This term also conveys a sense of deeper connection to God. A consolation is more than another way of speaking about happiness. Running marathons may be truly "consoling" to a soul, even though the physical discipline may be hard and stressful at times. "Desolations" are those feelings that bring a sense of distress, dryness, heaviness, or darkness. One feels a certain distance from God; prayer seems especially hard. For example, although your friend confidently declares that she is grateful for her good job—a vocation providing financial security and social benefits—she says that lately she is feeling lackluster during the morning commute. She describes her days as dry and heavy. Rationally, she doesn't know why she is distracted at work and fantasizing escape, but you begin to hear her heart contradicting the rosy picture.

Through faithful listening, spiritual friends can help each other hear the language of the soul. While completing my seminary studies, I felt a strong leading to continue graduate study in Christian spirituality. Weighing the pros and cons offered few practical reasons to spend another four or five years in school, though I knew that teaching was a crucial piece of my vocation. I was impatient to get involved in ministry. Evelyn Underhill seemed nearby, gently prodding me to follow my heart's longing, but the prospect of more schooling felt self-centered. Nevertheless, through the graceful listening of good friends, I began to feel the movement of the Spirit in wordless, deep consolations. It is still hard to articulate how I decided to continue my studies, but the spacious container of spiritual friendship enabled me to find a sense of peace and rightness about the decision.

Through faithful listening, spiritual friends can help each other hear the language of the soul.

We also need discernment for the inward spiritual journey. One of the gifts of a friendship grown in the soil of daily prayer and mutuality is the opportunity to compare notes. Where else can we regularly talk about our experiences of God, our spiritual practices, the times when praying is hard, and those shimmering moments of peace and well-being? The mutuality of friendship enables a back-and-forth flow of listening. Together both may drink from the same fount of many blessings.

Contemporary life provides precious little space for discernment, given the overriding burden of time. We hurry from one task to another, expressing thoughts and emotions on the fly but rarely sitting down to discern what they may be saying to us. Even accomplished multitaskers know moments of loneliness. In a quiet, predawn moment or while daydreaming between gulps of coffee at a traffic light, an ache may surface. We yearn to share the ordinary ups and downs of our lives with someone, the unspoken prayers we don't feel comfortable uttering at a church meeting, and experiences like the moment when we realized God had healed our heart after years of grieving a loss. Perhaps because of the emotional reserve that our society tends to demand of men, the ache men carry can be hidden under even deeper layers of conditioning. We all need the companionship of a loyal spiritual friend to discern where God is speaking or where God seems silent in our lives.

A spiritual friend can also help us to discern our blind spots, important for our ongoing spiritual formation. Celtic writer John O'Donohue describes the problem of solo self-reflection. It's like looking in a mirror: we can see the front of the body but not the back. The loving glance of a soul friend can help us honestly pay attention to that which is hidden from our conscious awareness.

One of the dark sides I unconsciously have carried into the light of spiritual friendship is a penchant for criticizing myself. One friend in particular helps me laugh at the subtle and not-so-subtle ways that my lack of self-acceptance arises. Sometimes when I am around this friend, I find myself stopping in the middle of a self-deprecating comment. She hasn't said anything; a look simply crosses her face, or a familiar gesture reminds me I have forgotten to love myself as I would my neighbor.

Blind spots are not limited to the unhealed places of our lives; we are also often prone to overlook our gifts, talents, insights, and beauty. With self-improvement being a commodity sold through advertisements and magazine articles and a title for an entire section in contemporary bookstores, we easily can fixate on what is wrong with us. Yet the mirror of a faithful soul companion can help us name the creativity and strengths God has placed within us.

> The loyal love of a spiritual friend may incarnate the word of God to us.

What the story of Ruth and Naomi teaches us about discernment is that over time the loyal love of a spiritual friend may incarnate the word of God to us. As with the spiritual discipline of *lectio divina* or the corporate practice of listening to a sermon, so it is that habitual and prayerful attention opens a space for us to hear the Divine. Through faithful spiritual companionship, we are able to sift the wheat from the chaff of our thoughts, desires, hopes, and fears. We may finally see truths about ourselves that have been long hidden, and we may discover what God is creating in and through our lives.

The Fruit of Loyal Love

The story of our widows ends happily. Naomi's strategy for betrothal sends Ruth to the threshing floor, where Boaz is winnowing barley with the others. Naomi directs Ruth to wait until Boaz has gone to sleep for the night, then to uncover his feet and lie there. When he awakens and finds Ruth, he will tell her what to do. Ruth does as her friend bids her, and when Boaz awakens, she quietly makes what is basically a marriage proposal: "I am Ruth, your servant; spread your cloak over your servant, for you are next-of-kin" (Ruth 3:9). Boaz is impressed by her loyal love, offered a second time, this time to him. He reminds her that there is another relative with closer ties but tells her he will meet this kinsman and seek permission to "redeem" Ruth.

Thus, with subtle political cunning, Boaz settles the matter and the couple marries. The joyful Naomi, only indirectly related by blood, becomes the doting grandmother. And the women in the village declare, "[Obed] shall be to you a restorer of life and a nourisher of your old age; for your daughter-in-law who loves you, who is more to you than seven sons, has borne him" (Ruth 4:15).

Among the many spiritual insights to be explored in this joyous turn of events, there are two that speak to the fruits of spiritual friendship. One is that Ruth's unfailing love for her friend is, in fact, more than a private and personal blessing; it changes the world! Obed becomes the grandfather of David, and for Christians, the ancestor of Jesus. Of course, God is not limited to the actions of one individual, and yet, what an incredible vessel Ruth becomes to further the gift of God. A second fruit borne of her loyal love is the transformation of her beloved mother-in-law, Naomi. Without guile, without economic power—but with boldness and great love—Ruth has given new life as well as economic security to an elderly widow for the remainder of her days.

A couple of years ago, a dear spiritual friend received a vision from God about taking a faith walk for peace, and after weeks of careful discernment the project became clear. She would walk over five hundred miles, from her home in Indiana to the nation's capital, declaring a simple message about seeking peace in our relationships, community, and world. Her loyalty to God amazed those of us around her; in spite of many obstacles she continued to take the next step in planning, just as she would later literally take steps on the road itself.

It was September, and the cornstalks crackled in the breeze, dry from the lack of rain that summer. Although I walked for only a few days with my friend during her six-week trek, I could begin to imagine the huge undertaking that Ruth and Naomi made, walking the long, dusty road from Moab to Judah. The pleasing bareness of midwestern farmland opened up for me in a way that freeway speeds formerly had occluded. Blackbirds sang to us from telephone lines, warning us not to bother the fields that belonged to them. The buzz of cicadas rose and fell in synchrony with the sun.

My friend's daily practice was to spend part of her walk in silent prayer, so as her footfalls kept a measured pace ahead of me, I felt my spirit relax into the rhythm. With the clutter of schedules and belongings gone, I experienced the interior rest of contemplative prayer. My feet were sore and my body wearied long before my friend's well-trained one, but the impact of this brief intersection with her pilgrimage ripened into fruit of inner peace for days afterward. Through my friend's faithfulness to her leading, and my devotion to her, the work of the Spirit in her life rippled into mine. And so it was for the many other friends and acquaintances who joined her, as well as church groups she spoke to and passersby who stopped to talk to her. Her walk of faith bore peace. Such is the nature of companionship in the Spirit; we join our companion walking down roads we never intended, and the roads become our own.

Sometimes the reverse is true; the project itself becomes a catalyst for friendship. Two friends of mine became spiritual companions out of their faithfulness to the social justice work of gleaning. Not unlike Ruth's time, contemporary farmers open their fields after the harvest to volunteers who gather the remaining produce and deliver it to the needy in their communities. My friends worked alongside each other in the fields for over a year before deep conversation began; they had been focusing more on the job at hand instead of talking to pass the time. Yet once earnest conversation began, the friendship flourished—and the two men began sharing parts of their life stories, their faith, and their dreams for the growth of the gleaning ministry.

In one of those serendipitous moments, they learned that they lived within five minutes of each other, a fact discovered in a field an hour and a half away from home. One friend invited the other to his church, which ultimately changed the second friend's life. Through this simple and heartfelt invitation, the second friend found a larger community in which he could develop spiritual friendships and continue the inner work he had begun in solitude. For both of them the freedom to share feelings, to express their love for Jesus, and to openly acknowledge their doubts about faith became the fruit of their "yes" to God. It was a "yes" to give time to gleaning for the poor and a willingness to risk that loyal love with each other.

As we have seen in Naomi and Ruth's story, friendships are born at the unique intersections of individual lives, be they serendipitous or through family alliances, common work, or volunteer service. Spiritual friendship, once born, is not simply passive attentiveness to one another; it is also—like all things birthed in God—a work of creativity.

Recalling Jesus' words to his friends in John 15, we too are called to bear fruit by abiding in the vine of Christ, the divine incarnation of *hesed* in the world. As you review the spiritual friendships in your life, where do you see the fruit-bearing vines? How do you tend the vines that extend through and beyond your friendship? Through what projects might you and your spiritual friend grow and give?

Consider projects that may deepen the spiritual walk of your friends, individually and corporately. You and your friend might take yearly retreats, hold a weekly Bible study, or engage in a spiritual discipline that you do together or individually. You may feel led to try a holistic approach that combines physical exercise with spiritual sharing. Two students in a summer course I taught practiced their prayer partnership by cycling together in the early mornings; they combined the meditative prayer of quiet pedaling with pauses to share moments of beauty, prayer requests, and spiritual insights.

In a prayer partnership I participated in as part of a discipleship course, my partner and I set a schedule of intercessory prayer that we each kept in our individual homes: Mondays, for her children; Tuesdays, for my nephews; Wednesdays, for a war-torn country we were concerned about; and so forth. I know that our shared commitment strengthened my faithfulness to intercessory prayer.

One or both friends may also experience a leading about a project bearing fruit for others. You and your friend may feel led to start a small group or teach a Sunday school class together. Perhaps your friend has long felt deep concern about literacy, and out of prayer with your friend, you decide to begin tutor training together. Perhaps you and your friend realize a common concern for learning the faith stories of elder members in your congregation, so you begin interviewing the elders and collecting their narratives in a booklet that can be shared. Many mission trips and community service projects are also birthed in conversations between faithful friends.

Small and powerless though they must have seemed to onlookers, the faithful journey of two widows to the elder's homeland would have ramifications affecting two major world religions. Nevertheless, even if we had only the first chapter of Ruth in our hands, still we would have one of the most beautiful testimonies to friendship love. Indeed, may we each hear again Ruth's vow of *hesed* to Naomi as a symbol of God's friendship love to each one of us.

CHAPTER 4

Jesus as Friend:
Kingdom Love

Jesus' earthly ministry may be viewed through many lenses. In addition to teaching and healing among the crowds and preaching on street corners, Jesus engaged religious leaders and mentored a group of disciples. He was a contemplative and a mystic—awakening early to pray and revealing the mysteries of God through parables. Jesus was also a sage, able to see into the hearts of those he encountered. Viewed through the lens of Judaism, his ministry was prophetic, part of a long line of prophets passionate to recover the heart of Jewish practice. As Christians, though, we are convinced that Jesus was more than a prophet; we exclaim along with Peter in Mark 8:29 that this one is indeed the Christ, the Messiah! Nevertheless, while beloved hymns celebrate our friendship with the Galilean, we may never have considered how Jesus approached friendship in his earthly ministry.

How did Jesus make friends? Did he befriend everyone he met? What qualities did Jesus value in friendship? What might he teach us about deepening friendships spiritually? Given Jesus' itinerancy, it is nice to know that he had at least one "home away from home" with well-to-do friends Mary, Martha, and Lazarus. We can imagine him showing up in Bethany for a few days, putting his feet up, and relaxing over dinner. Still, most of his closest friends were not of any means, nor were they religiously sophisticated. Jesus chose ordinary fishermen as his steady companions. And to make matters worse, as his critics loved to point out, Jesus was known to hang out with tax collectors, prostitutes, unclean lepers, the disabled, and other such sinners.[1] How could any upstanding Jewish male remain pure before God and blatantly eat with the unclean?

Jesus challenges us to extend the table of our friendships—to risk discovering a depth of mutuality and spiritual encounter with persons quite unlike us.

We may distance ourselves from these first-century prejudices, believing that we too would join Jesus in befriending outsiders. But Jesus' defiance of table fellowship rites is precisely what made his friendships so radical; he went against the social grain and challenged the ethical mores of first-century Palestinian Judaism. What conventions would he disturb today? If his approach doesn't make us uncomfortable, we probably are not paying attention to the unspoken rules of our own friendship circles. Sadly, I recognize that many of my friends look too much like me.

Now, I don't believe that Jesus asks us to forgo camaraderie with like-minded souls. Rather, he challenges us to extend the table of our friendships. He invites us to risk discovering a depth of mutuality and spiritual encounter with persons quite unlike us. We might begin by reaching out to someone of a different age or gender. Or we might widen our circle to include those of a different social status or of other cultures and faith traditions. Looking within the walls of the church, we might find ourselves called to seek friendships outside the labels we have clung to, such as conservative, liberal, or orthodox.

It seems unnecessary to add *spiritual* as a descriptor for Jesus' friendships; they were just naturally so. Perhaps as a youth Jesus played ball in the neighborhood and kept a low-key profile among his teammates. But by the time we meet up with him in the Gospels, Jesus doesn't waste much time on small talk. He ventures into soul territory in momentary encounters with others, just as he does with his three-year companions, asking questions we might hesitate to ask our best friend. The Gospels record Jesus' spiritual genius in these meetings, and while we cannot reduce his approach to a formula, we can note a few trademarks in his style.

First, we find that Jesus was awake to the moment and to the person before him. Second, he had a gift for asking the right question. Third, he spoke the truth in love, often in ways that we would deem impolite. True spiritual friendships emerged in those brief encounters, and we realize that Jesus was in the business of making friends all the time. We also begin to see that kingdom love was central to his befriending vision.

JESUS, THE SACRAMENT OF THE PRESENT MOMENT, AND FRIENDSHIP

Jean-Pierre de Caussade's eighteenth-century spiritual classic, *The Sacrament of the Present Moment,* illuminates a practice we instantly recognize in Jesus: deep awareness of the Divine in each moment. The Rabbi constantly invited his followers into nearness with God. In teaching his disciples to pray, he told them to call the most high God "Abba."

Jesus was awake to the moment and to the person before him.

Jesus did not separate his life into spiritual and secular components. He skillfully wove parables to illustrate this complementary vision, describing the kingdom of heaven as a tiny mustard seed that grew to be the tallest tree in the garden. Seeing with the eyes of Christ is surely the "participative seeing" that spiritual writer Tilden Edwards describes as being present to what is there "without finally separating from either the situation or God."[2] Jesus brought such participative seeing to all of his human encounters.

Members of the Religious Society of Friends, or Quakers, believe that the light of God is in everyone, and our task as Christ's followers is to answer the Inner Light within us and to foster the awakening of the light of Christ within others. Being available to Christ in each human encounter is a high calling, yet we can recall mystical moments in which we have indeed seen Christ in another person. I remember one moment distinctly. I was giving my infant nephew a bottle one evening and became aware of his gaze. Of course, I had looked into those eyes before, but this time his dark eyes were lively, piercing, and sweet. It seemed that his soul, fresh from heaven, was speaking to mine. His gaze became an icon of God's love for me. Even years later, the image remains vivid. However, staying awake in ordinary, everyday encounters is much harder, such as when I find myself in the grocery checkout line late in the afternoon. Do I really see the grocery clerk standing across from me, intent on making a speedy transaction, who is also bored, looking at her watch? What do I have to say to her, a person beloved by God? Or has she become the means to an end, one track closer on the errand train taking me home?

One depiction of Jesus is a familiar staple on Sunday school classroom walls: Jesus with children gathered around him, his face turned toward them in loving attention. Reading the story honestly as adults, we may feel empathy for the poor disciples. Perhaps they had already stayed in town longer than planned and needed to get on the road so they could make it to the next village before nightfall. Meanwhile, some parents are bringing their kids forward so Jesus can touch and bless them. That would have been fine a couple of hours ago, but the sundial isn't looking good now. Jesus, however, is indignant that his band of friends cannot see the gift of God in the moment. "Let the little children come to me," he says. "Do not stop them; for it is to such as these that the kingdom of God belongs" (Mark 10:14). His message is clear; the kingdom of heaven is revealed in the small and the unexpected. And it can be seen by those who are awake to the moment, just as children typically are.

Befriending in the way of Jesus is not a very Western practice. A dear friend, a retired missionary, describes the beauty of African meeting and greeting. In Nigeria, she recalls, greeting your neighbor is the most important thing you do. Being late to an appointment is not good. But if you meet a neighbor along the road and do not properly greet that friend, you make a more grievous social error. This may seem like a small interruption, but a proper greeting takes several minutes, as you should also ask about the health of all of your neighbor's relatives!

We get the sense that Jesus approached individuals in a manner similar to that of Africans, really seeing the person before him. In a pressing crowd, Jesus turns and asks, "Who touched me?" The disciples are stunned, but a trembling woman kneels before him, knowing she was healed as she touched the fringe of his clothes. "Daughter," he says gently, "your faith has made you well: go in peace" (Luke 8:45-48).

Like good listening, being truly present to the person before us is also a discipline, a spiritual practice. Often we are tired, in a hurry, worried about meeting a deadline at work, or perhaps distracted by the coffee stain on the white sweater we just bought. Yet we can hear Jesus' words to Martha, anxious about food preparation and her sister sitting at Jesus' feet as a disciple: "Martha, Martha, you are worried and distracted by many things; there is need of only one thing" (Luke 10:41-42).

While teaching English as a Foreign Language (EFL) at a community college several years ago, I felt God leading me to go to seminary. To confirm the direction of that call, I decided to do a semester of chaplaincy training at a local hospital. I visited patients on the weekends and some evenings and taught EFL classes during the week. In the beginning, I did not think my pastoral role was affecting my teaching; I just found myself on high alert at the hospital, worrying, *How do I witness to Christ's love as I visit the elderly woman in Room 4432? Did I talk too much when I was with the patient I just saw?* I also feared the prospect of seeing blood, worried that I might faint. Walking through hospital corridors, I prayed constantly before, during, and after my encounters with patients. Then, as the semester progressed, I discovered that I couldn't turn it off; the prayerful awareness followed me into the classroom. With students I began to hear myself saying inside, *How can I be present to this person, my student?* I was changing in a role that I had begun to take for granted. I was becoming prayerfully awake to my students in ways I had missed before.

What might it be like to walk through the day with prayerful intention about every person we meet, awake to the grace of those moments? What would it be like to encounter each one as a child of God, perhaps as a potential friend in God? In his book on spiritual friendship, *Anam Cara: A Book of Celtic Wisdom,* John O'Donohue describes the Celtic approach to finding soul mates as a kind of unceasing prayer. One walks through the day, he notes, praying to recognize those souls one is meant to meet.

THE GIFT OF THE GOOD QUESTION

Scientists, teachers, counselors, and spiritual directors all know the value of a good question. For the scientist, identifying the precise research question is critical to valuable data collection; a hypothesis is merely a tentative answer to the question that the experiment then checks.

Before becoming a graduate student, I privately believed that the Socratic method was an indirect, even lazy, way to teach; I much preferred a solid lecture. Then I had a professor who spent entire class periods asking thought-provoking questions. His insightful queries led the class into deep, engaging conversations of the topic at hand. I came to class better prepared, knowing that my brain would be exercised, and because my level of curiosity rose, I did learn more. Now that I teach spirituality, I have tried to design such questions, and I realize how hard it is! First, it is difficult to ask a question that doesn't have the answer in it (those "don't you think" kinds of questions). Second, it is a vulnerable feeling to see a discussion moving in a direction that you, as the teacher, have not prepared for. Finally, asking a question when you have a good version of the answer is humbling. Rather than showing what you know, you actively support students in discovering what they know.

Counselors also recognize the value of a good question, one that helps the client go deeper but doesn't interfere with the intuitive direction the individual's own process is taking. While having a different emphasis—the directee's relationship with God—the spiritual director also seeks to ask the right question, one that enables the directee to risk growing in the life of faith. Praying in the pauses, the director listens for the Spirit's direction about the focus, phrasing, and approach that the next question might take. The process is not always smooth, since the question arising in the director's soul may seem quite unexpected. Only afterward will the director realize that the question was wise and penetrating; in the moment he or she may wonder if it is crazy.

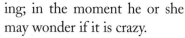

Jesus was a master of the kind of question that took a conversation deeper.

As we have noted, even in short encounters Jesus was a master of the kind of question that took a conversation deeper. Moreover, he deflected many questions, realizing that the issue behind the seeker's question needed to be explored, rather than an answer provided. In fact, he often directed a similar question back to the individual. Jesus' questions pushed his followers and friends beyond where they had been to honesty before God and themselves that was vulnerable, risky. Yet he knew that the right question could open the seeker to transformation, a new experience of grace, and a greater congruity of life and faith.

To an expert in the law who asks Jesus what he must do to inherit eternal life, Jesus returns the query, basically saying, "What do you think? What have you learned from studying the law all of your life?" (Luke 10:25-37, paraphrased). The lawyer responds with the commandments to love God with all of your being and to love your neighbor as yourself. And then, in an unconscious slip perhaps, the legal expert reveals his underlying worry, probably the real trouble he had: Jesus' mixing up the traditional rules about who should love whom. So he prods Jesus further: "And who is my neighbor?" Then Jesus tells the story of the good Samaritan, returning a similar but critically altered question to the lawyer, "So which one do you think acted as a true neighbor?" We can almost hear the guy choking out the words, "The one who showed him mercy." His legal mind could not help but state the truth, but he must have hated to admit that a despised Samaritan fulfilled the law better than two Jews who dutifully fulfilled the purity codes.

Jesus, again traveling in a crowd, hears the blind beggar Bartimaeus cry out, "Jesus, Son of David, have mercy on me!" Folks around Bartimaeus tell him to hush, but his cries get even louder. Just like the time he welcomes the children, Jesus' authority quiets the rebukers. With firmness Jesus reminds his followers to be available for God to the one you have been given, saying, "Call him here." When Bartimaeus reaches Jesus, we expect—no doubt like the crowd that was breathlessly watching—Jesus to do the obvious: heal the blindness. But with the acumen of a sage, Jesus simply asks, "What do you want me to do for you?" Bartimaeus replies, "My teacher, let me see again" (Mark 10:46-51). In his book *The Questions of Jesus,* John Dear notes that Jesus' question reflects the way God works with each of our souls.[3] God does not intrude, but in a servantlike gesture, the Divine waits upon the true answer welling up in our hearts. In asking the question, Jesus invites Bartimaeus to let go of his deepest wounds and give them to God for healing.

Taking Jesus with us on the road today is not an easy task. Even with our dearest spiritual friends we are rightly hesitant to be as bold as the Rabbi. It isn't our job to jot down a list of the ten most penetrating questions, ready to pull out as needed at our next meeting with our spiritual friend. Rather, we are called to follow the Quaker posture—one of waiting upon the nudging of the Inward Christ and then humbly asking the hard question. Most of the time our presence as listeners is what our friend needs. We help our friend by asking open-ended questions that allow him or her to shed the superficial layers blocking the answer that the Inward Christ is revealing.

Nevertheless, I know there are times when a spiritual friend has asked just the right question, a hard one. How, where, and who the question comes from are as important to me as the question itself. If the question comes from the latest self-help book my friend has read, I may take it seriously enough but also remember that my friend is not my therapist. More than likely, the real question will not be a popular or an expected one. It will come from a spiritual companion who has traveled a long way with me, and often it is one question among many that he or she has asked me. My friend may not even realize its importance until I reveal that it was, in fact, the question that went to the very root of the matter. I will also recognize it from the telltale signs in my gut. I trust questions coming from a true spiritual friend like the one Aelred writes about—one who is grounded in friendship with God, seeks my best, and asks the question in love. Perhaps the truest test is that my friend does not even know the answer, for it wasn't his or her question in the first place.

In a world where the pace of globalization is changing how we think about culture, religion, politics, and economics almost daily, it may be hard to comprehend the revolution Jesus began at the dinner table, where Jews excluded those of their own ethnic origin. My nephews wave to me from the highest tube at a McDonald's Play Place, and I smile at the sight of their playmates, children from a host of ethnic backgrounds. Enjoying the moment, I may forget the racial, social, religious, and economic problems that the United States and the American church still grapple with. Instead, I want to hope that the vision of Dr. Martin Luther King Jr.'s 1963 speech has come true, the dream that "children will one day live in a nation where they will not be judged by the color of their skin but by the content of their character." But sadly, I know better, and I know that the kingdom of God is still trying to grow into the tallest plant in the garden.

Even the narrative of Jesus' birth foreshadowed the radical nature of his kingdom message. Lowly shepherds were the ones chosen to receive the angelic message that born in Bethlehem, wrapped in swaddling clothes, was the long-awaited Messiah! Later Jesus would eat meals with such "people of the soil," the peasant farmers and day laborers who were despised as the pitiful rabble, ignorant of the law. Jesus would extend the table to include five thousand of these peasants gathered in a deserted place to hear him, his miraculous feeding reminiscent of God's provision of manna in the wilderness. The feast gave a foretaste of the fullness of God's kingdom, where all peoples will be integrated into a community of equals, and hunger will no longer be a daily concern.

The politics of Jesus and issues of spiritual friendship may seem only tangentially connected, but for Jesus they were intricately fused. Meals in first-century Palestine were not just times to eat together but highly complex events that reinforced boundaries, statuses, and kinship ranks. For an oppressed people who diligently kept meal regulations as part of their faithfulness to the Torah, Jesus' challenge could only be seen as subversive. Jesus' repeated table fellowship with sinners symbolically welcomed them into the community of the saved, and some biblical scholars believe that this was the last straw for the Jewish Sanhedrin. It was hard enough to have an external Roman threat without an internal menace.

What does Jesus' subversion of the purity codes mean for us today as we make friends and build communities? We each must ask that question prayerfully, reflecting regularly on lifestyle habits that exclude rather than include persons unlike us. It means taking to heart Jesus' practice of paying attention to the one before him, as he did with Zacchaeus the tax collector.

Tax collectors were particularly reviled because not only did they break the purity laws by mixing socially with Gentiles, but also they collaborated with their pagan oppressor by collecting taxes from their own people. As the chief tax collector, Zacchaeus was especially despicable because he gained his wealth from cheating his fellow Jews.

We read that Zacchaeus climbed a tree to see Jesus better, and it is remarkable that Jesus saw him at all. With eaglelike sensitivity, Jesus looks up, perceives the heart of this "lowlife," and invites himself to Zacchaeus's house (and to be sure, he would be eating with Zacchaeus as well!). The text says that all who saw grumbled, implying not only the Jewish leaders but also the "unclean," who found in Zacchaeus someone more despicable than they. Zacchaeus himself seems shocked. Even before he has had a conversation with Jesus, he repents: "Look, half of my possessions, Lord, I will give to the poor; and if I have defrauded anyone of anything, I will pay back four times as much." Jesus blesses his pledge of integrity of faith and social justice, declaring Zacchaeus's inclusion into the kingdom of God, "Today salvation has come to this house, because he too is a son of Abraham" (Luke 19:1-10). As illustrated in the story of the good Samaritan, Jesus makes the enemy the best of neighbors, part of the inner circle.

I like to think that I don't stratify or exclude others, that I seek to live in the way of Jesus, but internally I find myself judging. As a spiritual experiment one day in graduate school, I decided that I would drop all critical thoughts of others for an hour. *A piece of cake*, I thought. Within the first five minutes of class, I had already labeled three or four students, predetermining the value of their contribution to the class discussion. Suddenly I realized what I was doing, and I was appalled! I realized once again that being a Christian is not a matter of force of will; it is a moment-by-moment surrender to the Source. I, along with Bartimaeus, can only cry, "Jesus, have mercy" (Mark 10:47). Jesus reminded his friends—his disciples—that to be fruitful in their spiritual lives, they must remain attached to the Vine. Indeed, the prayer for mercy is a plea for reattachment, a prayer for strength in our very weakness.

My other problem is busyness; like the Emmaus road disciples, I worry about making the next village by nightfall. A few years ago, an unexpected friendship interrupted my busyness. Having taught EFL for many years, I have always been curious about meeting those from other cultures and faith traditions. The Quaker adage of seeing "that of God" in someone from another faith tradition is a working paradigm for me. One particular busy fall while teaching, I met a young Muslim woman, a teacher of Arabic from the neighboring college. One of my commitments to God after

September 11, 2001, had been to devote more time learning more about Islam and attending interfaith events, but like Augustine at the brink of his conversion, I found myself saying again yes, "but not yet." I was just too busy.

But this teacher refused to be politely distant. With joyful hospitality, she, a newcomer with a yearlong visa, welcomed me, among others, to her tiny apartment as if it were a grand, palatial home. When she invited me for the second time to an informal interfaith dialogue on campus, I could not say no. At those gatherings I was deeply moved by the depth of her testimony and her faithful spiritual practice. Whenever she spoke in my hearing, I found the Divine witness strong in her. Still, I didn't have time for a new friendship, and after all, she would only be close by for a year. When I felt too busy to reach out to her, it seemed as if God stopped me in my tracks and said, "Invite her to dinner!" I did, and we met more after that. In reflection, it is hard to fully express the gift that this devout Muslim gave me. It was she who was awake to the moment and aware of the one before her. Although from a different faith tradition, she actually breathed a breath of fresh air into my own Christian faith.

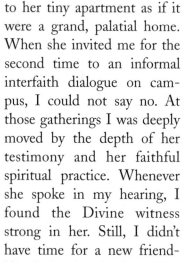

Jesus taught and exemplified a theology of friendship, a way of inclusion, a vision of the kingdom of God.

The memory of her befriending impulse continues to remind me that I need to stay awake to and consciously seek out the one who is unlike me. This is the theology of friendship that Jesus taught and exemplified: a way of inclusion, a vision of the kingdom of God. He asks each of us the same question, even as he shows the way to the answer: "Who is my neighbor?"

CHAPTER 5

Friendship with God: Longing Love

As Christians we are accustomed to thinking of ourselves as children of God or as sons and daughters of God. Most of us also feel at ease with our identity as servants of God. Nevertheless, we may find it hard to talk about ourselves as friends of God. We sing about our friendship with Jesus, but is it really okay to be on a first-name basis with God, the Almighty?

In our timidity, we can take strength from a humorous story told about Teresa of Ávila, who traveled by horseback across Spain in her efforts to reform the convents of her Carmelite Order. One day while crossing a river swollen with the spring rain, her party tried to float their supply wagons across on rafts. The ropes broke, and all of their provisions rushed downstream. At that point Teresa turned to God in frustration and heard an inward reassurance, "This is how I treat my real friends." To which Teresa replied boldly, "Then it's no wonder that your Lordship has so few!"[1] Even as we laugh at Teresa, we find a sense of rightness in her reverent but tenacious audacity.

So what does it mean to be a friend of God? We have looked at Aelred's vision of true spiritual friendship and the risking, loyal love in Ruth and Naomi's friendship. We've been inspired by the kingdom love of Jesus, whose friendship vision placed no boundaries on who was invited to dinner. Now, as we turn to consider our approach to friendship with the Divine, how might we describe it? I see it best as "longing love," a friendship that waits to be known fully. The mystics joyfully remind us that we are born from God; we live in God; and we return to God. Certainly we know this is true as we watch an orange-red sun drop beneath the edge of the ocean or witness a newborn kicking his tiny feet in the air. But so often these miracles of life are dimmed by distraction and busyness. We find ourselves stuck in the rut of the familiar. Our first Friend, God, may even seem far away.

We are not alone in this mix of emotions. The rich tradition of the communion of saints offers us companions in abundance who, like Teresa, knew times of dryness and spiritual apathy as well as seasons of ecstatic renewal. We can glean the fruit of contemporary psychology as well, which recognizes that untreated depression can fuel a despondency of soul. Or in terms of the body, we know that stress, lack of exercise, or other health problems intensify soul weariness. Reminders of death and diminishment may disturb our sense of God's nearness. Yet such seasons of dryness are part of a larger picture in which we as limited and precious human beings try to relate to Spirit and Mystery. It is natural to long for what we often cannot sense directly. The echo of Paul's words reverberates in our hearts, "For now we see in a mirror, dimly, but then we will see face to face" (1 Cor. 13:12).

We need the witness of spiritual mentors from the tradition to reassure us of God's befriending love. We also need spiritual friends here and now. Few of us are called to live the spiritual life as hermits. Abbots reserve this solitary calling for monks with years of community life under their belts. As embodied souls we live and move in a physical universe, and we need places to share our stories with other believers. We need opportunities to pray in common and to laugh, cry, and contemplate the mysteries of the spiritual journey with other travelers. How often I have been refreshed by the testimony of a friend who is experiencing the presence of God in a vivid way! I remember what I had forgotten. Later, savoring the conversation, I find hope returning that God is indeed near, even if my own kinship with the Divine has felt

We need the witness of spiritual mentors from the tradition to reassure us of God's befriending love. We also need spiritual friends here and now.

flat recently. For most of us, spiritual friendship with at least one or two others—as well as with communities of kindred souls—is a key aspect in renewing our friendship with God.

BEFRIENDING GOD THROUGH SPIRITUAL PRACTICE

A lively set of spiritual practices is also crucial to becoming better friends with God. Spiritual teachers in the East and West point out the benefits of a steady diet of practice as the way to open up the soul to the Other. It's hard to develop a friendship if you rarely spend time with your friend! Christian spiritual disciplines like *lectio divina*, examen, Bible study, spiritual reading, worship, and contemplative prayer afford us space to listen to our first and best Friend. Conversational prayer throughout the day, as well as breath prayers and the repetition of the Jesus Prayer, increases our connection to a gracious God who is invisibly near. We remember Brother Lawrence, who turned to God throughout the day even in the most mundane of tasks. At first he had to bring conscious effort to an ongoing awareness of God's presence, but over time it became a habit—the natural outgrowth of regular practice.

A lively set of spiritual practices is crucial to becoming better friends with God.

Grounding our spiritual disciplines is the story of Jesus' earthly pilgrimage in the Gospels. Jesus' friendship with God was revealed powerfully in the first spiritual practice we read about: a forty-day wilderness fast. There in the final, grueling days of desert hunger, Jesus wrestled with the dark side, and his faithful partnership with his Father was confirmed. We also catch glimpses of his ongoing friendship with the Father both in his early morning escapes to pray and in the mystical encounter at the Mount of Transfiguration. The vitality and joy he drew from this well of intimacy with God became manifest in his preaching, teaching, and healing ministry. While Jesus doesn't describe his spiritual practices in detail, we don't have to look hard to see the common ingredient: time alone with God.

Why is this return to solitude so necessary? What if I am outgoing by nature and find encounter with others, through conversation, the way I grow spiritually? Spiritual teachers like Teresa of Ávila, herself a raging extrovert, would say that solitude is a matter of addition to the spiritual life, not an end to communication with others. Teresa believed that knowledge of the self was critical to deepening the life of prayer. "We are incomparably stupid when we do not strive to know who we are," Teresa writes, "but limit ourselves to considering only roughly these bodies. . . . We seldom consider the precious things that can be found in this soul, or who dwells within it, or its high value."

Comparing the soul to a castle, Teresa goes on to say, "In the center and middle is the main dwelling place where the very secret exchanges between God and the soul take place."[2] Teresa did not mean to suggest that interiority was noble in and of itself. If we are always looking within, we can become fixated on grudges we are carrying or worry endlessly about a nagging fear. Or we can become preoccupied with ourselves and apathetic. Yet in the quiet recesses of the heart we can begin to hear ourselves think, and once we begin to let go of thoughts, move into a deeper posture of receptive prayer. Here in the silence, Quakers believe, we can sense the stirrings of the Inward Christ or Inner Light; we can hear what God in Christ is saying to us.

But solitude is not the same as sitting in silent meditation (though it may mean just that), nor is it to be confused with isolation. Flora Slosson Wuellner describes a helpful contemplative practice she calls a "parable walk."[3] She invites her readers to take a walk in nature with the purpose of listening for God's intention and voice through the experience. The parable walker may take a problem or concern with him or her or simply be open to receive a "word for the day." Listening through the five senses is key to this practice. A sparrow's playful delight in the underbrush may remind a grieving student of God's infinite tenderness. Or a young woman worrying about a nagging problem may see a little boy fall on the sidewalk and run to the comforting arms of his parent, where he is soothed by empathy and kisses. As a bystander of the little drama, she may be flooded with an awareness of God's nearness and care.

The first time I went on a twenty-four-hour silent retreat, I was nervous. Could I stand the quiet for that long? Everything went fine the first evening and the next morning. At the retreat center, there were stations with icons, clay, and art materials. And I kept busy. In the morning I spent time writing in my journal. At meals I relaxed and enjoyed eating meditatively. However, after lunch ended on the second day, I felt the panic rising again: *Another four hours without talking; what will I do?* I decided to take a walk and try the only thing I thought I could do: let go! I had to let go of the time, the fretting, and certainly my control of the experience. Climbing over the ridge of a hill, I suddenly felt the breeze whoosh through the pines. Since childhood I had sensed God's nearness through the wind. The cool sharpness of the air seemed to instantly clear my head of its anxious clutter. I was filled with gladness, the kind of smiling joy you have when you remember a good joke. After this came a deep sense of well-being. Some years later, I would hear a famous line from Julian of Norwich that expressed this feeling: "All shall be well, all manner of things shall be well." This indeed was my sense of God's friendship that afternoon, a gift made possible through exterior quiet.

REFLECTING ON THE TRINITY:
A MODEL OF DIVINE FRIENDSHIP

Theology—or thinking about the nature of God—may not always be given the attention it deserves in discussions of the spiritual life, but the two are intimately connected. If, for example, I perceive God as a judgmental parent who is waiting for me to shape up, I will have trouble relaxing and being myself in God's presence. If I think that God is interested only in the "big stuff"—like international conflict and global warming—my own personal longings, hopes, and fears may feel unimportant. Or if becoming better friends with God might mean that I will be called to do something I hate, I may prefer a distant, once-a-week approach to the Divine. Theology is to be found every time we relate to God. In fact, it is good to think consciously about our theology in order to deepen our relationship with God.

Over a lifetime, we internalize beliefs about God; some we can reaffirm later in life, and others we cannot. I may have fixed a certain view of God in the eighth grade that now at midlife no longer works. Conversion in its fullness is an ongoing, lifelong process. As we do in human friendships, we also experience feelings of frustration, anger, and disappointment in our friendship with God. Even as we acknowledge the holiness of our Divine Friend, it is still important to be honest with God about these feelings, as the psalmists do time and again. "I say to God, my rock," the psalm writer cries out, "'Why have you forgotten me? Why must I walk about mournfully because the enemy oppresses me?'" (Ps. 42:9). In a human friendship, if we are unable to express

Just as we do in human friendships, we experience feelings of frustration, anger, and disappointment in our friendship with God. It is important to be honest with God about these feelings.

hurt and disappointment, we will find the relationship becoming superficial. Likewise, in friendship with God, who knows the human heart intimately, we are invited to be ourselves, even as we are called forward into greater fullness and love.

Considering the nature of God, we find a model of divine friendship in the theology of the Trinity. This may surprise us, since human triangles can be dicey. We remember that lesson from the playground. If there were two or four kids, the chance of evenhanded play was better than if there were three. Two children might overpower the third, or one might lord it over the other two.

Thankfully, the Trinity is a vital, healthy, and creative triangle. Unlike the territorial tendencies of human threesomes, the Trinity is a dynamic interflow of love and reciprocity. There is no possessiveness or jealousy. Creativity is lavished without ownership, and love is offered without bargain. It is a friendship in which joy knows no bounds. Each member of the Trinity innately represents the nature of the other members. In fact, it would be impossible for these Divine Friends to do otherwise.

A Russian icon of the Holy Trinity, painted by Andrei Rublev in 1425, expresses the Trinitarian connection. The icon shows an intimate conversation of three angels around a table. Each figure has an open posture toward the others, with fingers gesturing symbolically about the shared divine project of salvation. In *Behold the Beauty of the Lord*, Henri J. M. Nouwen describes how prayerful meditation using Rublev's icon invites us to dwell in "the house of love." "Through the contemplation of this icon," Nouwen writes, "we come to see with our inner eyes that all engagements in this world can bear fruit only when they take place within this divine circle."[4]

Likewise, Jesus pointed to this wellspring of love in the

divine friendship in the fifteenth chapter of John's Gospel.[5] There Jesus invited his followers, whom he now blessed as his "friends," to enter into a dynamic relationship with the divine life. The analogy Jesus used is a familiar one in the Hebrew scriptures. Yahweh is represented as a vinegrower and Israel as the grapevine. Reconfigured in Jesus' poetic teaching in John 15, the vinegrower is still the Father, but Jesus himself has become the "true vine." Every branch— that is, every believer—receives its lifeblood through porous fibers connected to the Vine. "Abide in me as I abide in you," Jesus tells his friends. "Just as the branch cannot bear fruit by itself unless it abides in the vine, neither can you unless you abide in me" (15:4). Jesus describes the juice that flows through this grapevine alternately as love and obedience. Jesus abides in the flow of his Father's love by keeping his Father's commandments; we, Jesus' friends, abide in him, and therefore in the Father, by fulfilling the commandments of Jesus. Jesus explains that all of these commandments may actually be summarized as one: "Love one another as I have loved you" (v. 12).

Obedience may seem foreign to the notion of friendship, but it need not be. To obey is to listen and respond, to yield in love to another. Yielding to the love of his Father, Jesus discovered joy. There was no begrudging compliance in Jesus' relationship to God. Such is the way of mutual love among the members of the Trinity. Typical understandings of power and obedience are turned upside down. For it was through his ongoing process of yielding in love to the Father that Jesus received the energy and passion for his earthly ministry. And so Jesus invites us, his friends, to experience this same joy by yielding to this same love, incarnated in him, our Teacher and Redeemer. Quite simply, Jesus says to his disciples and thus to us, "I have this wonderful kinship, and I want you to share in it. It will bring you such joy." Filled with this divine love, we will bear the fruit of love for one another. And so Jesus describes what Aelred would later conclude: that our spiritual friendships with one another are made possible only by abiding in Christ.

In my own experience of friendship with God, Jesus' revelation of his Father's character enables me to trust, to risk, and to hope in a Mystery I cannot see. Of course, the Old Testament contains many compelling revelations of God's compassionate brooding over creation, as well as God's faithful covenantal love with the Hebrew people. But it is by watching Jesus, who received children and outsiders alike, that I deepen my trust in a compassionate, faithful Creator. Through Jesus I know a God who accompanies all of us even through the greatest of sufferings. A dying friend described his surrender to this divine Mystery as something akin to being led blindfolded "because there seems to be no knowing what will come next." Nevertheless, he wrote in a final letter to his friends: "There also seems to be little fear in walking a path that God has walked before me."[6] While I have yet to face the immediate prospect of death—the ultimate risk of trust in friendship with God—I can imagine yielding in that final moment to the unending mercy of divine love so vividly portrayed in Christ's life. Because of Jesus, I can trust that the table of eternal divine friendship has been extended to include even me.

Abiding in the Vine

In his analogy of the vineyard, Jesus portrayed the mystical grace of Trinitarian love, a mystery that defies easy explanation. Moreover, Jesus reassured his friends, he had not left them alone because the Advocate, the Spirit, would come to guide them into all truth (John 15:26; 16:13). Through the Spirit we also rely on a wealth of New Testament and spiritual writings, the lives of saints, and many spiritual practices that have been handed down. All of these tools help us abide more deeply. We also experience mystical revelation ourselves, moments when dwelling in the house of Trinitarian love becomes real to our human understanding.

One such experience happened for me on a crowded bus in mainland China in March 1984. My friend and I had arrived the month before to teach English in a small college on the outskirts of Beijing. China was still emerging from the Cultural Revolution, and in those early days I was still coming out of my own case of culture shock. We were on our way into the city with a list of errands and the prospect of lunch with another American. Tired and homesick, I swayed with my garlic-eating traveling companions as we jerked along the uneven road; the unpleasant smell of "night soil" wafted

Experiences of God's presence in and through nature reveal the divine friendship to us.

in from the early spring fields. The thought I had been suppressing all morning would no longer submit to my will. *What in the world am I doing here?* my heart cried out. There, in the pause that followed, I felt myself enveloped by a sensation of love and peace. The bus still rocked; the irritating buzz of an unfamiliar language still rang in my ears; but I knew all was well. God's abiding presence was filling me. My fears drained away, and I was left with compassion for those around me. The remaining months in China would become joyful and deeply rewarding.

Experiences of God's presence in and through nature also reveal the divine friendship to us. A few years ago, a student described to me such an awakening. It happened during a stressful time, the end of a long semester—and then came the unexpected news of a fellow student's death. Restless and sad, she decided to take a walk through the woods on the back campus one warm spring evening. She could hear the wind and the birds, then slowly an indescribable sound that grew louder and louder. She began to sense that the chirping sound was coming from frogs, singing not just in the pond in front of her but also in the puddle next to her. Gradually she realized that the chirping was rising from the grass all around her. Lingering for a while, she let the sound fill her. It grew dark and she turned for home, walking slowly, cupping her ears to hear the frogs as the sound grew fainter and fainter. Still she could hear them singing. In this moment of joy, she realized that had she not filled herself with their sound and then paid attention to it all the way home, she would never have recognized their sound from a distance. The experience became a living parable, one renewing her sense of God's immanent love. Like this student, we too are called to cup our ears and listen for the echoes of our Friend's voice through a sometimes-silent heaven.

Partnering with God in the World

As we spend time with a dear friend, over time we may begin to pick up, as marriage partners often do, mannerisms and even aspects of our friend's disposition. One particular spiritual friend of mine is bubbly and joyful, and after a few hours with her, I begin to see the world with greater awe and wonder.

As we spend time with our Divine Friend, we also find our sensibilities shifting, our ways of being in the world changing. Priorities and values that once had top billing recede to the bottom of the list or vanish altogether. Quaker mystic and spiritual writer Thomas Kelly describes this transformation: "We are torn loose from earthly attachments and ambitions—*contemptus mundi*. And we are quickened to a divine but painful concern for the world—*amor mundi*. [God] plucks the world out of our hearts, loosening the chains of attachment. And He hurls the world into our hearts, where we and He together carry it in infinitely tender love."[7]

In Paul, the enthusiastic church planter and New Testament theologian, we witness a vigorous partnership with God that transformed Asia Minor into a seedbed of Christianity. For Clare and Francis, the lure of divine friendship called them out of their lives of ease into kinship with the poor of this world, those whom Jesus had declared to be rich in the kingdom of God. Evelyn Underhill, brought up in a nominally religious home, found her heart set ablaze by a fire to know God through her reading of Christian mystics. Her friendship with God led her to write over thirty books on the spiritual life. Just as our spiritual companions affect us, so God's friendship invites us into partnership that extends Christ's vision of kingdom love into the world.

God's friendship invites us into partnership that extends Christ's vision of kingdom love into the world.

During the seventeenth century, English Christian "Seekers," suspicious of the outward formalism of the state church, began to gather in silence to experience God inwardly as both Spirit and Truth. George Fox, dissatisfied with the lack of spiritual fire among state-supported clergy, searched for a way to cross the gulf between human and Divine. One day while reading scripture, Fox experienced a sense of the real presence of Christ. He heard an inner voice saying, "There is even one, Christ Jesus, that can speak to thy condition." As Fox began sharing this message of inward revelation with others, Seekers began to join him, calling themselves Friends of Truth, Children of the Light, or simply Friends. They identified themselves with the disciples in John 15, who were called out of servanthood into a partnership of friendship with Christ. This movement of Friends, popularly called Quakers, grew through these inspired meetings, where individuals waiting in silence for the word of the Inward Christ might quake in response to the intensity of the message they were led to speak.

The story of the Religious Society of Friends, a group small in number but large in witness, is inspiring. American Quaker John Woolman exemplified the powerful effect that even one person could have if he or she operated out of intimate friendship with God. As a child in the New Jersey colony, Woolman was grounded in Quaker practice and scripture. He also encountered God's love deeply in creation. It became evident to him that surrender to divine, universal love was the only way to "regulate" the "temper and conduct" of each of us in regard to all other creatures. Indeed, such love might call us to act "contrary to present outward interest," "thereby incurring the resentments of people," yet opening "the way to a treasure better than silver and to a friendship exceeding the friendship of men."[8]

John Woolman was led to act contrary to eighteenth-century Quaker tolerance of slavery as well as to their ownership of slaves. At age twenty-three while working for a merchant, Woolman found his conscience in great turmoil as he wrote up a bill of sale for an African woman slave. He would never do that again, and after years of prayerful searching, Woolman felt led to "travel in ministry" through the colonies, pleading lovingly among Quakers to free their slaves. He continued this ministry of persuasion, traveling one month out of every year, until he died from smallpox at fifty-one. Woolman did not live to witness the abolition of slavery; nevertheless, by 1787 no American Quaker owned a slave, largely due to his efforts.

Ruth's spiritual friendship with Naomi led her to leave the land of her birth—all that was familiar and secure. And so friendship with God calls us beyond the comfortable and the known. As partners with God in the world, we enter into a working friendship with the Trinity. Of course, we will be stretched, but we may forget that this stretching takes us deeper into the house of love. Buoyed by our Friend's inspiriting juices and feeding at the table of endless mercies, we take the next step on the path that is ours in particular to follow. Perhaps, like Woolman, the nudge forward will come as a prick to our conscience, or perhaps as a still, small voice.

Friendship with God calls us beyond the comfortable and the known.

The echo of Jesus' counsel in John 15 reminds us that only by abiding in the Vine of divine love will we discern and then find the courage to do that which may be difficult in the very next moment to do.

Some persons seem to experience an accelerated partnership with God in the world, which becomes evident to us as we study their lives in retrospect. The "Little Flower"—Thérèse of Lisieux, a French Carmelite who died of tuberculosis at the early age of twenty-four—recorded an autobiography of profound inward and outward grace. *The Story of a Soul* describes the journey of someone on a spiritual "fast track." In a letter to her sister Marie, she wrote about her meditation on the story of Jesus and the Samaritan woman. In her interpretation of Jesus' request for water, Thérèse sensed Christ's deep desire for our friendship: "Ah! I feel it more than ever before. Jesus is parched. . . . He finds few hearts who surrender to him without reservations, who understand the real tenderness of his infinite love."[9] Thérèse realized that while great deeds were not possible in cloistered life, she could offer small deeds of sacrificial love to Jesus. She performed many acts of kindness in secret. Thérèse acted so loving toward one ill-tempered sister that the latter asked Thérèse why she liked her so much!

For Etty Hillesum, a woman in her late twenties, a deep sensitivity to God intensified as outward reality was stripped from her. Nominally Jewish in her Dutch upbringing, Etty found herself on a profound spiritual journey in the early years of World War II. Her inner life was then transformed in a transit camp in Nazi-occupied Holland. As she offered compassionate care to her fellow Jews, Etty drank daily from the wellspring of God that was within her and fed regularly from the Gospel of Matthew. From early in the morning until late at night, Etty tended the sick, comforted those waiting for the dreaded weekly transport, and offered a "shining" presence of imagination and love to the inmates.[10] In a letter to a dear friend a few months before her death, Etty shared some lines from her diary:

> You have made me so rich, oh God, please let me share out Your beauty with open hands. My life has become an uninterrupted dialogue with You, oh God, one great dialogue. Sometimes, when I stand in some corner of the camp, my feet planted on Your earth, my eyes raised toward Your heaven, tears sometimes run down my face, tears of deep emotion and gratitude. At night, too, when I lie in my bed and rest in You, oh God, tears of gratitude run down my face, and that is my prayer. . . .

Things come and go in a deeper rhythm, and people must be taught to listen; it is the most important thing we have to learn in this life.[11]

Even though our lives may seem outwardly secure, friendship with God cannot help but lead to transformation. As we are led deeper into love, we begin to see the ones God loves with greater compassion. For some of us, this friendship love may even require sacrifices we cannot now imagine. Jesus knew the ultimate risk of friendship when he told his followers, "No one has greater love than this, to lay down one's life for one's friends" (John 15:13).

CHAPTER 6

Getting Started:
The First Hurdle

As we have seen, spiritual friendship is rich and multi-faceted. While a profound gift of grace, friendship also requires faithful tending to grow in healthy, meaningful ways. In this chapter we will explore some of the practical realities of beginning and sustaining a spiritual friendship.

As we considered earlier, Aelred of Rievaulx describes some timeless ingredients of spiritual friendship, such as right intention and loyalty. Nevertheless, his context was a monastic order. Although these communities weren't always serene, they certainly were less hectic than the worlds most of us inhabit today.

For most of us, each day involves choosing among several good activities. A typical weeknight might bring such decisions as "Do I have time to work out at the gym before dinner?"; "I wonder if I should spend time tonight on the Internet researching that problem at work"; "Oh, I need to make those calls about our Sunday school class picnic"; "We can't wait much longer to clean out the fridge because some 'science experiments' are already underway"; and "Oops, I almost forgot, tonight is the first class in the series on deepening your spiritual life that I signed up for at church!" On and on goes the list—our crowded days and multiple roles make far too many worthy time demands, and we soon realize the limits of our energy.

Friendship requires faithful tending to grow in healthy, meaningful ways.

Thus, it is not surprising that friendship, especially the care and feeding of an intentional spiritual friendship, gets neglected. It's not that we don't care about our friends or that we don't want to foster the kind of eternal spiritual kinship that may be ours through Christ. It's just hard to find the time! A related issue arises around our mobile culture. If I make the investment in a spiritual friendship and my friend has to move away because of a job change or family issue, will I be left high and dry? Is it worth a possible loss to invest so much of myself now?

Without denying the real problem that full schedules demand or the work that distance requires of friendship, we underestimate the power of prayer and intention in relationship building. In Jesus' earthly ministry, we witness a busy teacher and healer walking through villages, reaching out with loving intention toward countless individuals. I believe these brief, holy encounters were spiritual friendships all their own. Moreover, some of the persons he encountered joined his intimate circle of disciples.

We therefore see in Jesus' ministry a shorthand method for making spiritual friends. What if I followed his lead and took this week as an experiment in praying daily for spiritual friendship in my life? I might find the face of an acquaintance coming to mind, one with whom I shared a meaningful conversation at the office Christmas party but never followed up with. Or I might be led to sit down and write a letter to a dear friend who moved to another city two months ago. Or as a friend of mine did several years ago, I might call together a circle of women (or men) for a spiritual friendship group meeting once a month. Or I might have a leading to call the Guatemalan friend I made on that Habitat project last summer to ask about starting a prayer partnership.

Practically, friendship begins within. Just as with taking up any spiritual discipline, we need to discern whether we are willing to invest our hearts and lives in a particular friendship we have an inclination toward. This may mean inviting the prospective friend to coffee or lunch—not to interview him or her for the role, but as an opportunity for both to listen to the ways God is calling us. Many folks are loving and faith-filled, but we may find little heart affinity with them or have difficulty being ourselves once we spend more time together. Not all friendships are meant to grow into long-term spiritual friendships. As in all of our loves, there are factors we cannot determine before being in the relationship.

Yet we must be careful not to decide impulsively against a particular spiritual friendship just because the other person has a different temperament or life experience.

Not all friendships are meant to grow into long-term spiritual friendships. Yet we must be careful not to decide against a particular spiritual friendship just because the other has a different temperament or life experience.

Discernment requires prayerful listening within, then looking for signs of a genuine encounter with the other. These signs might include a certain resonance, a desire to learn something together, a hope that arises spontaneously, or a sense of joy and ease in the relationship. You may feel as if you have known the person much longer than *chronos* time would suggest, or you sense that you have much more to discover in the friendship.

Given the trial-and-error that all good friendship entails, it may be hard to be honest with ourselves about fears that the relationship might not work out. As Ignatian practices would encourage, we should test the consolations and desolations we feel. Apparent differences may hide the potential for discovery and growth on both sides. I know that I have experienced this truth in a loving friendship of many years. While I am an introvert and often shy about initiating conversation with new people, one of my dearest friends has never met a stranger. I often joke with her that I have had many lessons in hospitality and extroverted care just by being in her company. Over the years, I have also seen her steady heart and wise spiritual reserves. In turn, she has appreciated my quiet, faithful presence and listening. Had we judged the difference in our personalities as an impediment to greater depth, we might have missed a significant friendship that God was opening before us.

THE QUESTION OF BOUNDARIES

In Celtic thinking, two souls may be attracted to each other spiritually, just as two persons experience physical attraction. In retrospect, we see how often this is true. Engaged in conversation with a new acquaintance, we sense a natural camaraderie, or a joy, a liveliness of spirit, is enkindled. We find ourselves asking, like the two disciples who joyfully realized that it had been Jesus with them on the way to Emmaus, "Were not our hearts burning within us while he was talking to us on the road?" (Luke 24:32). Nevertheless, because such soul attraction can be emotionally compelling, we have all the more reason to discern carefully the calling of the particular relationship. As we saw in chapter 1, there are good reasons to pause around the question of boundaries as we consider the next step.

One boundary we are well aware of in the workplace but may overlook in church and other religious communities relates to power, particularly the power assumed in pastoral and mentoring roles. Hopefully this power is not used for personal aggrandizement but for God's service; still, it makes demands. If I am called to a congregation as a pastor, my situation is similar to serving in a teaching or counseling role—I will need to cultivate friendships of depth and mutuality outside the congregation. Likewise, when I mentor a youth or befriend a child, my first obligation is always the well-being of the young person. While it is good to admit to youth that adults make mistakes and to share some of the mixed feelings that come with being human, we are, in fact, the ones with more power and privilege in the relationship. We must find healthy adult friendships outside of these unequal relationships of spiritual nurture for our own needs to be expressed. Such wisdom seems like common sense, but as rapport deepens, power (with its advantages and responsibilities) can be minimized.

Sexuality is another issue we can ill afford to forget in spiritual friendship, even as we acknowledge the beauty of a friendship like Francis and Clare's. Embodiment is ever a gift to the life of the soul, but it also requires prayerful tending. The passion that mystics experience for God, as well as the spirituality inherent in sexual expression (both positive and negative), teaches us that sexual desire likely will arise naturally around feelings of spiritual intensity. Yet even if both spiritual friends are available for a romantic relationship, a love relationship may or may not be what God is inviting. If there are other boundaries, such as relationships of marriage or long-term commitment, then the discernment becomes even clearer. We decide to stay awake and to honor each other's primary commitments. Even with prayerful awareness, feelings may resurface from time to time.

In addition to self-reflection on the questions around sexual desire and spiritual friendship raised in chapter 2, it is good as a matter of spiritual hygiene to name feelings or concerns regularly with a spiritual director or mentor outside the friendship—well before fantasies of recklessness invade. This does not mean divulging the confidences of our friend, nor does it mean we should become anxious every time feelings of sexual attraction arise. When such feelings begin to distract us, a thoughtful spiritual director can guide us to notice how God may be inviting us into deeper communion with the Divine or to pay attention to our overall sexual self-care. He or she can also help us to notice when we are getting "into trouble," perhaps not in the relationship itself yet, but within our own psyches and souls.

Sometimes feelings and desires—appropriate in the right context—will begin to interfere with the friendship itself. We should carefully bring up the issue with our friend and prayerfully discern if the friendship can continue. It is vital to do this with the knowledge of a mentor, director, or mature spiritual friend outside the relationship. We may subconsciously be seeking confirmation for our feelings from the friend in question and be unprepared for the detachment (and so feel ourselves to be unlovable) or for the return of feeling ("Let's pursue these desires and longings in secret"). Accountability to a spiritual director or friend will help us remain honest about the long-term consequences of acting on the feelings and/or support an intentional process of ending the friendship.

GOING DEEPER

There is no single recipe for creating and deepening a friendship. If you think about the friends you have made in your life, you will probably find as many different approaches as friends! Nevertheless, there are a few tried-and-true practices that help a spiritual friendship to flourish. The first one returns us to the question of juggling priorities. For a friendship to grow, we need to carve out regular times to meet and give these meetings priority on our calendars. We may decide to meet once a month, setting aside two hours to get together in a quiet setting, or we might meet weekly for breakfast on Thursdays. Or as spiritual companions wanting to incorporate exercise, we may arrange to meet twice a week to walk for

For a friendship to grow, we need to carve out regular times to meet and give these meetings priority on our calendars.

thirty to forty minutes. Regularity helps provide a "container" for the relationship; we begin to internalize the rhythm and, unconsciously, prepare for the encounter. Like the practice of other spiritual disciplines, the habit itself provides the grounding for the gifts that emerge.

It is also important early on to name what each of us believes to be important in the friendship. As Aelred noted, loyalty is key to any spiritual friendship. One way that friends show loyalty is through keeping confidences.

While this concern may seem obvious and discussion about it stilted, naming the issue clearly can spare hurt and disappointment later. If, for example, I have a spouse or partner, I may be tempted to share something with him or her learned through conversation with my spiritual friend. Saying aloud to my friend that I will not share details, even with my spouse, strengthens the container for the friendship and reminds me to be faithful to my promise. Hearing it from my friend will also likely free me to take risks in sharing.

Perhaps because monastic life is framed with prayer, Aelred does not mention its centrality to spiritual friendship; nevertheless, prayer is an essential foundation. Often a spiritual friendship is birthed in a community of prayer, such as a prayer partnership begun out of a Bible study group. Thus, the habit is woven into the fabric of the relationship. However, if the friendship has a more casual beginning, conversation about how prayer frames the relationship becomes more important. Two friends may decide to ask each other for prayer requests to carry between get-togethers, or they may take time to pray aloud for each other at the end of their mutual sharing. Perhaps the pair begins their monthly meetings in silent prayer, allowing consecration in Christ to temper and deepen the sharing. Others may put together a variety of prayer approaches, trusting the spontaneity of the Spirit to guide them.

Friendships also tend to adopt ritual patterns, sometimes because of conscious intention from the start, other times emerging as the friendship takes its unique form. In one of the spiritual friendships I cherish, we meet weekly—first checking in, then doing *lectio divina* with psalms and readings, and finally praying out loud together. My meetings with another friend occur every three to four weeks. After a light lunch, we take time to center in silence and then begin sharing, first one and then the other, out of that sacred space. When the weather permits, we might take a walk and then stop and focus for a time in silent worship. Often one of us will initiate the sharing of prayer requests that we take with us between get-togethers.

As we explored in the chapter on Ruth and Naomi, kindred souls may find one another while gleaning fields or while participating in a mission trip, community project, or church commission. On the other hand, friends who have met primarily for the intention of prayerful sharing and mutual support may need to listen for a vision that calls the friendship into action beyond the relationship itself. Intercessory prayer, Evelyn Underhill points out, is the closest thing to "absolute action," and two friends may be led to pray regularly for an orphanage or government leader for a time. Two other friends might feel called to go on a pilgrimage together to witness the mission work of their denomination and find specific ways they might become more involved. Friendship in and through Christ, the true Vine, will bear fruit. As spiritual friends we are called to support the other in the ways that Christ is calling each of us individually; we are also called to listen for leadings that may be ours to do together.

Laughter and play belong in spiritual friendships, as do rest and renewal.

Laughter and play, gifts that childhood friends know well, belong in spiritual friendships, as do rest and renewal. We often put off taking personal retreats perhaps because the solitude feels too lonely—or too many other activities and projects cry out for our attention. By planning a retreat with a long-term friend, we are more likely to keep the commitment as well as support the other in the spiritual discipline itself. We might agree to a gentle schedule of silence, sharing, worship, and rest. For example, on one retreat, my friend and I agreed on silence until the evening meal, when we shared thoughts that had arisen for us during the day, and then took a walk together before a simple evening worship. The retreat turned out to be deeply restorative because of the silence and the prayerful sharing that my friend and I scheduled into our day.

TRANSITIONS AND LOSSES IN SPIRITUAL FRIENDSHIP

Having moved between both coasts before I was twelve, I thought I would be comfortable with transitions by the time I became an adult—but they are still challenging. How do I fully unpack my belongings and embrace the gift of the new, while also staying connected to the individuals and communities I have left behind? Happily for many of us, e-mail and cell phones have become vital communication links across time and space, although the occasion of a personal card or letter is a special delight.

Rituals of leave-taking, planned reunions and homecomings, and the precious link of prayer help us navigate these passages, for we know that change and loss are inherent in friendship. Death is a reality that all friends face; even soul mates die. We need to take time to grieve the loss of dear friends. Nevertheless, Aelred contends, spiritual friendship is not limited to our present, embodied state; it may come into its greatest joy after death. Should one friend die, the other may continue to "joyfully partake in abundance of the spiritual fruit of friendship, awaiting the fullness of all things in the life to come."[1] Moreover, through prayer, Aelred notes, we may experience a mysterious communion with our friend through Christ, until that day of eternal reunion.

In Celtic understanding, one's *anam cara* should be present at one's death. This is a tall order, given the complex networks of relationships we have in the modern world as well as the distances that divide us. I was given the privilege of being with a soul friend near the time of her death. After months of prayers and efforts (diet, affirmations, and the work of believing) for her healing, those of us in her friendship circle had a party to celebrate her birthday. She was only partially aware, but love radiated from her eyes and she slurred words of delight as she looked at each one of us. Several days later, I sat by her bed, offering presence and attention while her husband went on his first outing in weeks. She slept or tossed and turned. Then suddenly she sat up straight in bed, looked me in the eyes, and asked, "Stephanie, am I going to die?" It was not a question I had planned for, but I knew I could not offer false hope. As gently as I could, I told her that

It is important to periodically reflect on the gifts we receive from each of our friends.

it looked like she might die. With a sigh, she lay down again. Stroking her hand, I watched as she fell into a deeper sleep, perhaps feeling more peaceful; I'll never know. I wondered if I had done the right thing, but I was given a sense of calm about my decision. Two days later she died. I had witnessed a moment of spiritual friendship from which I could not turn.

In the ordinary loss of everyday changes, we may not so reverently partake of the spiritual fruit of our friendships. It is important, then, to periodically reflect on the gifts we receive from each of our friends. We should review the lessons and insights we have gained because of their loyalty and patience. Through the practice of examen, we might record these gifts in our prayer journal or share them directly with our friends as a spiritual practice. Birthday cards, e-mails, and letters provide other opportunities to name the gifts of the other. Let us not delay in doing such practices of love, one to another, for such is the way of the kingdom of God.

Notes

CHAPTER 1

1. Patricia Loring, "The Centrality of Listening," *Friends Journal* (August 1997), 8.

2. Ibid., 9.

CHAPTER 2

1. Aelred of Rievaulx, *Spiritual Friendship*, trans. Mary Eugenia Laker, vol. 5, Cistercian Fathers Series (Kalamazoo, Mich.: Cistercian Publications, 1977), 61.

2. Ibid., 51, 53.

3. Ibid., 74.

4. Ibid., 115.

5. *Francis and Clare: The Complete Works*, trans. Regis J. Armstrong and Ignatius C. Brady (New York: Paulist Press, 1982), 203.

6. Carol Lee Flinders, *Enduring Grace: Living Portraits of Seven Women Mystics* (San Francisco: HarperSanFrancisco, 1993), 27–28.

CHAPTER 3

1. This phrase comes from a beautiful poem by Marge Piercy, "The Book of Ruth and Naomi," found in her book *The Art of Blessing the Day: Poems with a Jewish Theme* (New York: Alfred A. Knopf, 2000), 102.

CHAPTER 4

1. In first-century Palestine, *sinners* referred to those unable to keep the purity codes. Sin was seen as anything that made one impure before God. Sinners included those who were unable to fulfill the cleanliness rituals in the law, as well as those not considered whole: persons with skin diseases, eunuchs, the disfigured, the chronically ill, and the disabled. According to this belief system, if a person was poor, the reason must be a lack of righteousness before God. To read more about the purity system and Jesus' challenge to it, see Marcus Borg, *Meeting Jesus Again for the First Time: The Historical Jesus and the Heart of Contemporary Faith* (San Francisco: HarperSanFrancisco, 1994), 50–58.

2. Tilden Edwards, *Living in the Presence: Spiritual Exercises to Open Your Life to the Awareness of God* (San Francisco: HarperSanFrancisco, 1994), 45.

3. John Dear, *The Questions of Jesus: Challenging Ourselves to Discover Life's Great Answers* (New York: Doubleday, 2004), 9–10.

CHAPTER 5

1. Flinders, *Enduring Grace*, 174.

2. Teresa of Ávila, *The Interior Castle*, in *The Collected Works of St. Teresa of Ávila*, vol. 2, trans. Kieran Kavanaugh and Otilio Rodriguez (Washington, D.C.: ICS Publications, 1980), 284.

3. Flora Slosson Wuellner, *Prayer and Our Bodies* (Nashville, Tenn.: The Upper Room, 1987).

4. Henri J. M. Nouwen, *Behold the Beauty of the Lord: Praying with Icons* (Notre Dame, Ind.: Ave Maria Press, 1987), 21.

5. While the church did not formally adopt the doctrine of the Trinity until the fourth century, Jesus explores the divine life in terms of Father, Son, and Holy Spirit in the farewell discourses of John's Gospel.

6. Steve Ackley, personal letter, December 2005.

7. Thomas R. Kelly, *A Testament of Devotion* (New York: Harper & Row, 1941), 47.

8. *The Journal and Major Essays of John Woolman*, ed. Phillips P. Moulton (Richmond, Ind.: Friends United Press, 1971), 46.

9. Margaret Dougan, "Thérèse, A Latter-Day Interpreter of John of the Cross," in *Experiencing St. Thérèse Today*, vol. 5, Carmelite Studies Series, ed. John Sullivan (Washington, D.C.: ICS Publications, 1990), 101.

10. See Jan G. Gaarlandt, introduction to *Etty Hillesum: An Interrupted Life: The Diaries 1941–1943 and Letters from Westerbork* (New York: Henry Holt & Company, 1996), xxi.

11. *Etty Hillesum: An Interrupted Life*, 332.

CHAPTER 6
1. Aelred of Rievaulx, *Spiritual Friendship*, 131.

About the Author

Stephanie Ford is assistant professor of Christian spirituality at Earlham School of Religion in Richmond, Indiana. She holds a BA and an MA from Oral Roberts University, an MA from Oklahoma State University, an MDiv from Baptist Theological Seminary at Richmond (Virginia), and a PhD from The Catholic University of America.

While rooted in the Baptist tradition, Stephanie has been fed by Methodist, Catholic, charismatic, Episcopal, and Quaker traditions. In 1994 after several years of teaching English as a Foreign Language to college students,

Stephanie returned to seminary, where she studied with E. Glenn Hinson. She continued with doctoral studies in spirituality at The Catholic University of America. Stephanie's dissertation focused on the theology of Evelyn Underhill, the gifted Anglican spiritual writer.

At Earlham School of Religion, a Quaker seminary, Stephanie teaches on the topics of prayer, spiritual direction, the history of Christian spirituality, small-group guidance, and the relationship of spirituality to the body. She also leads retreats and has written for publications that include *Weavings: A Journal of the Spiritual Life* and *The Upper Room Disciplines.*

Stephanie's hobbies include reading, traveling, ballroom dancing, and playing the piano. She and her husband, Les Williams, have recently adopted a little girl from India—a delightful addition to their family.

Other Titles of Interest

Under Her Wings
Spiritual Guidance from Women Saints
by Kathy Bence

Under Her Wings explores the stories of five renowned women from Christian history and presents them as spiritual guides for today: Madame Jeanne Guyon, Teresa of Ávila, Thérèse of Lisieux, Catherine of Siena, and Julian of Norwich. Bence invites the reader to spend ten days "under the wings" of each of these women, benefiting from their insights and experiencing God in new ways.
ISBN 978-0-8358-0943-6 • 224 pages • Paperback

The Art of Spiritual Direction
Giving and Receiving Spiritual Guidance
by W. Paul Jones

In *The Art of Spiritual Direction,* you'll discover the answer to these questions and more:
- What is spiritual direction?
- What is the difference between spiritual direction and counseling?
- How can you know if you are called to the ministry of spiritual direction?
- What should happen in spiritual direction sessions?

Spiritual director and author Jane E. Vennard calls *The Art of Spiritual Direction* "the most comprehensive book available on Christian spiritual direction. Jones gives the reader a full understanding of the various types of spiritual direction as well as guidelines, methods, and resources for sessions."
ISBN 978-0-8358-0983-2 • 312 pages • Paperback

To order, call 1-800-972-0433 or visit us online at
www.upperroom.org/bookstore